STEMMING T

"None of us can ever start living a Christian life in a good world; we all have to live in history where good and evil are inescapably intertwined."
>> Richard K. Ullmann: *Between God and History*

Notwithstanding all the immeasurable ignorance and stupidity of the majority of the race, there is a gradual and sensible victory being gained over barbarism and wrong of every kind. I think we may, in some sort, console ourselves. If we can't win as fast as we wish, we know that our opponents can't in the long run win at all.
>> John Bright, Quaker Member of Parliament (1843-1889), writing to his sister.

Things fall apart; the centre cannot hold;
Mere anarchy is loosed upon the world,
The blood-dimmed tide is loosed, and everywhere
The ceremony of innocence is drowned;
>> W. B. Yeats: *The Second Coming*

Stemming the Dark Tide

Quakers in Vienna 1919-1942

by
Sheila Spielhofer

William Sessions Limited
York, England

© Sheila Spielhofer 2001

ISBN 1 85072 267 6

Printed in 10 on 11 point Plantin Typeface
from Author's Disk
by Sessions of York
The Ebor Press
York, England

Contents

Chapter		Page
	Glossary	vii
	Introduction	x
	Prologue	1
1	The Dying City	4
2	A Quaint Assortment	22
3	Prophetic Vision	40
4	Quaker Faith in "the Age of the Buttonhole"	52
5	A New Jerusalem?	64
6	Political Unrest…	75
7	Despots, Dictators and Despair	84
8	A Work Camp in Marienthal	90
9	Austria Abandoned	99
10	Darkening Skies	106
11	Conscience and Confusion	122
12	Darkness Falls	140
13	Closing the Doors	148
	Epilogue	161
	Bibliography	164
	Index of Names	169

List of Illustrations

	Page
Singerstrasse, showing No 16 on the left. (old postcard)	10
Second from Right seated: Hilda Clark, showing the effects of poor food and overwork c. 1920. The older girls in this Austrian children's home are learning hygiene in order to combat tuberculosis (CLARK FAMILY ARCHIVE)	10
Three-year old Viennese children with rickets caused by undernourishment 1920	12
Hilda Clark recuperating in Kaltenleutgeben (CLARK FAMILY ARCHIVE)	34
Rudolf Böck in the garden of his house, which became the home of the first Viennese Quakers (VIENNA MEETING)	73
Undergraduates helping unemployed Austrians to prepare the ground for vegetables and medicinal herbs in Marienthal 1936 (DENNIS CONOLLY)	96
Cambridge graduate being seen off at the station near Marienthal (DENNIS CONOLLY)	96
Bernard Lawson with his wife, Mary. He never lost faith in the Vienna Group even in the darkest days (CHRIS LAWSON)	101
Staff members at the Vienna International Centre Summer 1938 Front Row seated from left: Elizabeth Yarnell; Emma Cadbury; Ethel Haughton; Standing: Robert Yarnell; Mary Campbell; Hubert Butler; Brigit Kelsey Hodgkin. The two Austrian workers, Käthe Neumayer and Franz Lipovsky, are not shown. (VIENNA MEETING)	107
Jewish doctors learning to do manual work at the Quaker workcamp in Kagran in preparation for emigration to South America. August 1938 (RUTH KARRACH)	114
Ruth Karrach's passport, issued to enable her to leave Austria with the *Kindertransport* (RUTH KARRACH)	118
Jo Schindler, the gentle Viennese Friend, with his assistants, at the children's home he helped to found for child victims of the second world war (SHEILA SPIELHOFER)	137

Glossary

AFSC	American Friends Service Committee
Anschluss	economic and political fusion of Germany and Austria
ARA	American Relief Administration
Arbeitsausschuss	executive committee of German Quakers
Bad Pyrmont	beautiful old spa, site of oldest Quaker house in Germany
C.I.S.	Council for International Service
Clerk of the Meeting	person chosen to preside over a Quaker meeting and keep the minutes (see: Meeting)
FE&WVRC	Friends Emergency and War Victims Relief Committee
F.I.S.U.	Friends Union of International Service
FHL	Friends' House Library, situated in the Quaker centre in London
Foreign Membership Committee	set up by British Quakers to register new members in Europe
Friedensstadt	"peace town", name given to a new housing development in Vienna after the first world war
Friends German Emergency Committee	London committee formed by the Quakers to help refugees from Nazi Germany
German Yearly Meeting	denotes the whole body of German Quakers and their annual conference. Since the *Anschluss*, it also includes Austrian Quakers

Heimwehr	Austrian right-wing paramilitary organisation
Konfessionslos	not belonging to a recognised church
Kristallnacht	Nazi pogrom euphemistically called "the night of crystal glass"
Kinderfreunde	Socialist organisation providing education and leisure activities for children
Kultusgemeinde	Jewish religious community in Austria
Land Settlement Scheme	Housing development scheme in Austria to provide people with small family houses and gardens in which to grow food
London Yearly Meeting	denotes both the whole body of British Quakers and their annual conference (now replaced by Britain Yearly Meeting and Ireland Yearly Meeting)
Meeting for Business	session to decide on Quaker affairs
Meeting for Sufferings	executive committee of London Yearly Meeting, originally formed to help members in distress, especially those in prison for their convictions
Meeting for Worship	Quaker devotional meeting
Neue Hofburg	part of the Imperial town palace in Vienna
Quäkerspeisung	programme for feeding school children in Germany after the first world war, administered by the AFSC
Religious Society of Friends (Quakers)	official title of the religious community. The terms "Friend" and "Quaker" are used interchangeably
Republikanischer Schutzbund	social democratic paramilitary organisation
SCF	Save the Children Fund

Schönbrunn	Imperial summer residence in Vienna
Ständesstaat	"corporate state", name given to the form of non-democratic government in Austria under Dollfuss
Vaterländische Front	organisation to replace the free trade unions, after the Dollfuss government had abolished democracy
"weighty" Quakers	wise and experienced Quakers whose opinions carry special weight

Introduction

SHEILA SPIELHOFER has produced a magnificent book. She has utilised her excellent story-telling skills and mixed them with the fruits of assiduous research to cast an enormous and complex story into a highly manageable and readable form.

She outlines the changing contexts in which Quakers in Vienna found themselves between 1919 and 1942 with just enough detail, resisting an over-complex analysis, and then places the lives of so many fascinating and courageous Friends and friends of Friends into that picture. We get to know in a vivid and vital way people such as Hilda Clark, Alois Jalkotsky, Francesca Wilson, Carl Heath, Rudolf Böck, Emma Cadbury, Rudi Böck, Käthe Neumayer, Grete Sumpf and begin to understand what drove them in their work for the visions they held so dear. The stories of 'Cows for Vienna' or Jack Hoyland's 'Franciscan Battle Plan' and the workcamp at Marienthal are told with a humour and an optimism, reflecting that of those who set the schemes up, whilst not marginalising the suffering that schemes such as these were seeking to alleviate.

'Stemming the Dark Tide' is a history of Quakers in Vienna during these difficult and continually uncertain years, a story of many of those who lived and worked through those times, seeking to build peace in its widest sense, and a reflection of the complex attitudes of British and American Quakers to relief and mission in the 'interwar' years. It also illuminates the tragic history of Austrian Jews after the Anschluss and challenges and complements Schmitt's work on 'Quakers and Nazis.'

It is a story of imperialisms and identities. It begins in an Austria coming to terms with terrible financial and material hardship and suffering in 1919, but also with the loss of the huge Austro-Hungarian Empire, in which Austria was the dominant partner, and all the status, wealth and power that entailed. Fifteen years later, democracy within the new republic is suspended by Dollfuss, and a few years later, Austria is annexed by her German neighbour to become merely the 'eastern district'. The allied powers that imposed the crippling financial blockade in 1919 simply allowed this to happen. In some ways, Austria never had the chance to find its own sense of democracy or its own sense of nationhood. Even in the 1920s, 'red Vienna', with its Settlement programme and then the People's Palaces, was out of tune with the rest of the nation. Different imperialistic forces played their interests out on Austrian soil to an everchanging sense of what it was to be Austrian (and Sheila is excellent at drawing out fundamental differences between the Austrian and German character).

Then there is the Quaker imperialism. British Quakerism after the first world war found itself in a new place. The sense of self-importance as a civilising influence in the world 'alongside Empire', so well documented by Brian Philips in his doctoral work, had been replaced by a critical attitude towards a British government which had resorted to conscription in 1915. In 1918, London Yearly Meeting adopted its nine points of social order in a peak of socialist zeal which was to prove increasingly uncomfortable in the following decades. At the time of the General Strike in Britain in 1926, articles were appearing in the 'Friends Quarterly Examiner' which claimed that the Yearly Meeting had perhaps been over hasty or naive in its pronouncements at the end of the war. It was also a Yearly Meeting seeking to re-envision its mission work, and it is relief work in the later twenties which melded a theoretically apolitical activism with an ongoing sense of mission and service. The disagreements which Sheila draws out so well between the ideas of Hilda Clark and those of Carl Heath were those of the early 1920s and reflected the then-divide within London Yearly Meeting.

Only personalities and differences of structural allegiance, not different senses of Quakerism, keep the Vienna Quaker International Centre and the Quaker Meeting there apart in the later years. Whether Austrian Friends should be part of London or the new German Yearly Meeting becomes an issue for the Vienna Quaker group, whilst the Centre continues to be run from outside that group. At the same time, the Centre itself becomes a site of contested loyalties and visions, between the more relief and service-oriented vision of Headley Horsenaill and Emma Cadbury and the 'spiritual' agenda of the German Hans Albrecht and American Douglas Steere, a division settled in favour of the latter group and resulting in the Centre's closure in 1942. On the ground, AFSC personnel and British Friends worked together well but from far-away head offices, differences were more obvious, a fact which is directly related to the different political contexts in which Quakers in Britain and the USA found themselves in those years. Whilst British Friends reassessed the nature of their witness in the twenties, resulting in swings first in one direction, then in another, the newly formed AFSC had a greater sense of confidence and optimism, borne of two and a half centuries of being a political player within the USA, and of a exciting sense of new Quaker unity after the schisms of the nineteenth century. These differences then played themselves out on foreign soil, in this case, Austria.

But this is a book also full of hope. Using a rich array of primary sources, located and researched over a number of years and in a number of locations, Sheila Spielhofer as itinerant scholar draws out the optimism which sustained so many of the characters we read about in the face of so many reasons to perhaps give up. Useful psychological insights as to people's motives and behaviour aside, we are allowed inside the driving visions and read of the dedicated and selfless work undertaken to achieve them.

It is then a book which is fundamentally important to us as we, too, live in a time when war, totalitarian governments, and economic sanctions continue to produce so much suffering. It is a world in which Quakers still feel called to service. Even though this service has been increasingly institutionalised and professionalised, the lives we read about here are examples to us all. And the questions raised about the nature of service and mission remain ones for Quakers worldwide today. In the end, all is service, though: service to a humanity in need. This book is both a history and an inspiration in this regard.

Ben Pink Dandelion
Pendle Hill, April 2001

Prologue

THE ASSASSINATION on 28th June 1914 in Sarajevo of the heir to the Austrian imperial throne, Archduke Franz Ferdinand, by Serbian nationalists took Austrian ministers by surprise, but they soon saw it as a good opportunity to strengthen Austria's position in the Balkan countries and challenge the influence of Russia in that area. They hoped that the assassination could be put to good use to mobilize public opinion in favour of war. An ultimatum delivered to Serbia on 23 July made such extreme demands that it was indignantly refused by the Serbs, as had been intended. Having been assured of German support, Austria declared war on Serbia on 28th July, exactly a month after the assassination.

The various peoples of the Austro-Hungarian Empire had not much say in the matter. In all the other lands that took part, even in Czarist Russia, the declarations of war which followed were confirmed by their Parliaments. Only in the Austro-Hungarian Empire was the assent of the people not even sought.[1]

In Germany, whose leaders had been looking for just such an opportunity, mobilization was ordered at the end of July, ostensibly in order to support Austria, whereas Russia, France and England opposed her. Later Italy joined the forces opposed to Austria, after receiving promises of substantial gains at the end of the war. The passionate nationalism which greeted the war in all these countries surprised most of the leaders. The young Winston Churchill warned the House of Commons in a prophetic speech that

> when mighty populations are impelled on each other, each individual severally embittered and inflamed, when the resources of science and civilization sweep away everything that might mitigate their fury, a European war can only end in the ruin of the vanquished and scarcely less fatal dislocation and exhaustion of the conquerors. Democracy is more vindictive than Cabinets. The wars of peoples will be more terrible than the wars of kings.[2]

However, like the Austrian government, the leaders of most of the hostile countries expected that the war would be of short duration, and they concentrated all their resources on equipping the army with weapons, neglecting the need of both the soldiers and the civil population for food and clothing. Moreover, both Germany and Britain tried to weaken their enemies by attempting to get control of the sea routes and the passage of merchant ships.

As far as Austria was concerned, the blockade led to an increasingly desperate food shortage, which began to undermine the discipline of the troops. The harvest of 1916 was poor. With the death in the same year of the old Emperor Franz Josef, who had reigned for more than sixty years, opposition to the war increased. Although his successor, Emperor Karl, promised widespread reform, the common people were more concerned about the lack of food than political considerations. With the Russian Revolution of 15. March 1917 and the entry of the United States into the war on 6th April 1917, demands for self-determination increased within the Austro-Hungarian Empire.

In January 1918, after President Wilson in his "Fourteen Points" had suggested autonomy for the subject nationalities, a cut in flour rations set off a wave of strikes in many towns in the Empire. In Styria, a unit of Slovene soldiers mutinied, shouting, "Up with the Bolsheviks, long live bread!".[3]

A few months later, after the final Allied breakthrough and even before any armistice had been signed, large numbers of soldiers from the non-German-speaking provinces of the Empire formed themselves into groups of compatriots and simply turned their backs on the war, making their way home to support the founding of their new nations. Austrian officers were frequently forced to realize that they had no control whatsoever over the troops that were still nominally under their command.[4]

On 11 November 1918, an armistice was declared. The following day, a Republic was proclaimed in the small remnant of the Empire which was now Austria. The allies, fearful that Austria would follow Russia's example, made any plans for relief supplies dependent on Austria's rejection of a Bolshevik-style revolution. In the first general election in February 1919, the Austrian Social Democratic Party, which had adopted a policy of social reform within a democratic framework, won by a small majority. In an attempt to stabilize the country, they formed a coalition government with the right-wing conservative party, which called itself the Christian Socialist Party.

Vienna was in chaos and the people were on the verge of starvation, but there was no fighting. The city was now surrounded by new states hostile to their former capital. In the agricultural districts of Austria itself, the big landowners and the peasants were equally suspicious of "Red Vienna", which was under the control of the Social Democrats, and refused to send it food.[5]

Even after the armistice had taken effect and all fighting had ceased, the allies kept up the food blockade of Austria and Germany in order to ensure that both countries would agree to the terms of the peace treaty. The victors eventually imposed very harsh terms on both Austria and Germany, including the payment of huge indemnities to enable Britain and France to repay their debts to the USA. In 1923 the Society of Friends, whose members had opposed these harsh terms from the beginning, issued an *Appeal to Peoples and Rulers*:

> On financial, economic and political grounds, the Treaty of Versailles has been arraigned. We, however, are burdened chiefly by its fundamental immorality. The first consideration for the framers should have been to relieve the common suffering of the peoples rather than to increase the power of victor States. It was wrong to exclude the conquered from the Peace Conference, wrong to impute sole guilt and to extort an admission of that guilt by the weapon of starvation, and it was wrong to ignore the promise of better terms to a democratic Germany. The treaty is morally invalid because many of its provisions, unjust in themselves, are a breach of the terms on which the Central Powers laid down their arms.[6]

By that time, however, the harm had been done. The terms of the separate treaty concluded with Austria at St Germain-en-Laye on 10th September, 1919 were so crippling that they set the small country on a course which could only lead to further disaster.

NOTES
[1] Braunthal 1935:69.
[2] Bartlett 1984: 88.
[3] Braunthal 1935: 71.
[4] Interestingly, one casualty of this situation was Ludwig Wittgenstein's brother, Kurt, who in October or November shot himself when the men under him refused to obey his orders. See Monk 1990:11.
[5] Fry 1926: 194.
[6] Hasley 1938: 5.

CHAPTER 1

The Dying City

NOT EVEN THE most pessimistic Austrian could have foreseen the extent of the disaster which struck the country at the end of the first world war. It was reduced from a large and prosperous Empire to a small country of six million inhabitants, much of its arable land and industry had been lost, and its people were starving. The Emperor had renounced all participation in state affairs, although he never formally abdicated, and political upheavals shook the country.

When the Quaker doctor, Hilda Clark, set up her headquarters there in the autumn of 1919, almost a year after the armistice, Vienna, with its huge buildings and beautiful parks, still looked like the centre of a huge Empire. But everywhere there were queues of pale, thin people, huddled into old, patched army coats, waiting for their pitifully small rations of wood or bread. They were so resigned to their fate that Hilda Clark sometimes felt that an outbreak of violence would be easier to bear than this hopeless acceptance of such dreadful conditions, although her Quaker convictions, as well as her common sense, told her that nothing would be gained by that.[1]

Hilda Clark was the youngest daughter of Helen and William Stephens Clark from the Clark shoe-manufacturers in Street in Somerset. She grew up in an influential and affluent Quaker family. From early childhood, she imbibed the ethos of service to the community which characterised many of the Quaker families of the nineteenth century. Her parents encouraged her to find the work best suited to her character and allowed her a measure of independence unusual for the time.[2] Thus, unlike many other talented young women in pre-war England, she had the means, as well as the confidence, to pursue a worthwhile career.

Following in the steps of her aunt, who was one of the first women doctors in England, Hilda chose to study medicine. Just after she had qualified as a doctor in the summer of 1908, at the age of twenty-seven, three decisive incidents occurred in her life, which probably paved the way for her future commitment. First of all, she had a narrow escape from death, which seemed to her family miraculous, when she was thrown from her pony cart and dislocated her neck. A woman passing by found her unconscious, with her head at a strange angle, so she gently pulled it into place.[3] The second of these events was a truly tragic one. The first death certificate which she signed after qualifying was that of her friend and sister-in-law, Cara, who died in childbirth, with Hilda Clark sitting at her bed-side, unable to help her. These two events cast a "spiritual glow" over the summer, which to her was "made more perceptible than normal by such things as a narrow escape and the advent of a baby...I feel as if my whole life might be better and more use to others from those two days, but what an awful price it is to pay...And if I ever again have to hold such a cold hand and feel such a death-stricken pulse, I think a little of the love I have for Cara will go out to the victim, whoever it may be".[4] The third decisive event was that her sister, Alice, fell seriously ill with tuberculosis, and Hilda took charge of her treatment, under the supervision of an expert on tuberculosis. This experience was of great value later on in her work in Vienna, where she actively co-operated with the well-known Viennese doctor, Pirquet, who was a pioneer in the field of treating tuberculosis, especially in children.

The following September, she took up her first post in a maternity hospital in Birmingham. She also began to play an active role in the suffrage movement. Like most Quaker women, Hilda Clark found nothing strange in the idea of equality between men and women, since, from the beginnings of Quakerism in the seventeenth century, such equality had been recognised within the Society, at least in theory. Now that women began to demand equal civil rights, however, even many Quakers did not give them support. Hilda Clark threw herself into the campaign to change these attitudes with characteristic determination. Her courage was tested during the election campaign of 1910, when she spoke at meetings in the poorer districts of Birmingham. Although the police were there, ostensibly to keep the peace, she was pelted by men in the audience with fish and fowl heads and intestines, as well as with tomatoes and "many less-recognisable dainties", as she put it.[5]

When the first world war broke out, her first reaction was to propose that Friends should set up a special committee to find ways of relieving the sufferings of the civilian populations in the war-torn areas, as they had already done during and after the Franco-Prussian war (1870-1871).[6] She was supported by a Quaker Member of Parliament, T. Edmund Harvey. The committee, known at first as the "War Victims Relief Committee (France)", met in the basement of Hilda Clark's house in London and received the immediate backing of the London Yearly Meeting.[7]

At first, she also planned to go as a doctor to Serbia, but she admitted to herself that her interest was in "the wider issues of peace rather than medical work" and she wanted to be a "civilising and anti-war influence".[8] Instead, she went to work in war-torn France, organising relief work and setting up hospitals for women and children there. She admitted that she had at last found what seemed to be her real calling and wrote, "I am thankful to have at last a comparatively straight path".[9]

With her friend, Edith Pye, who was an excellent nurse and organiser, she instituted the Châlons Maternity Hospital, which was at times in the thick of the fighting between the German and French armies. At one point, when the shelling became too intense, the hospital had to be evacuated, and the women and the new-born babies were taken for safety to the champagne cellars near the town. Usually, the mothers who filled the hospital were solid French housewives, but there were sometimes tragic cases, like that of a thirteen-year-old girl who had been raped by a drunken soldier and who was brought to the hospital by her distraught parents several months before the baby was due, because they did not know how to cope with the child, who seemed dazed and out of her mind. The mothers at the hospital took her under their wing and taught her to look forward to the joy of having a baby, so that, after the baby was born, she was able to return to her parents, happy and well and able to care for it.[10]

The success of this hospital led to Hilda Clark being asked by the French authorities to organise several similar ventures, so that for four years she worked unceasingly, setting up hospitals and convalescent homes throughout France. She had obviously discovered that her real vocation was in planning and setting up well-functioning organisations. To her sister she confessed to feeling "supremely happy to be really at work" and wrote, "though I should prefer definite work like the others to the plotting and planning and interviewing that falls to my lot, things are much pleasanter than they were. It is still rather groping in the dark in a foreign tongue".[11]

That a woman should be in charge of such large scale relief work was certainly an innovation, even for Quakers. In the earlier relief work in France (1870-1875), most of the "field commissioners" were men, while the women were usually responsible for organising and packing the relief goods in England. Those who did venture into the field, did so for limited periods of from one to three months.[12]

As well as the physical danger and the innumerable practical difficulties that Hilda Clark and her fellow workers had to face, there were also spiritual ones, as she recorded in a letter written from Châlons in April 1915:

> The standing up for peace in the midst of the machinery of war, while owing our lives and the scope for work to those who are

fighting, the strain of work in the midst of intense personal sorrow and anxiety, of wondering whether it would be better to enlist, of a hundred doubts – it is all this that is at the bottom of difficulties which on the surface appear to be superficial practical ones that someone is to blame for...[13]

By the time she was finally able to lay down all these responsibilities in the summer of 1918, she was utterly exhausted and looked forward to a few peaceful months in which to recover her health. However, it was soon clear that the end of hostilities did not mean that true peace had been restored to Europe. A new task presented itself to Hilda Clark, when she heard of the plight of the starving peoples in the former "enemy" countries.

She first went to Vienna in May 1919 at the request of General Smuts,[14] who had stayed in Vienna a few weeks earlier while on his way to negotiate with the Communist leader of Hungary, Bela Kun. A huge meal was put on in his honour by the head of the British military mission in Austria, Sir Thomas Cunninghame. General Smuts was furious and called it a "serious lack of taste". He ordered that all his entourage should eat only army rations so as not to take away food from the starving people, whose sufferings had obviously made such an impression on him that he could not rest until something had been done to alleviate them.[15]

Soon after her arrival, Hilda Clark wrote home to say that the cries of the beggars in Vienna were almost more difficult to bear than the constant shelling that had formed the background to her work in France. Obviously, the situation in Vienna called for the same kind of organising skills. Having seen with her own eyes the pitiful condition of the starving population, especially the children, who were always her first concern, Hilda Clark went back to England to report to the Friends there and to convince them of the necessity for sending immediate help. She resigned from her position as Health Officer in Portsmouth and prepared to return to Vienna as soon as possible.

The Viennese were not just on the verge of starvation, but actually starving. During the winter months and up to April 1919, the population had existed mainly on cabbage and turnips. Thousands of children lived on half a litre of vegetable soup a day, with no fat or protein in it, which they obtained from public kitchens. Even in the hospitals, the food was about one-fifth of a normal diet. To the misery of the lack of food was added an acute fuel shortage. Austria no longer had access to its former coal fields in Poland and Czechoslovakia, and the Germans, who might have been disposed to help her, had to sell their coal to wealthier customers in order to pay off the enormous indemnity imposed on them by the terms of the Treaty of Versailles. There was not even enough fuel to heat the hospitals. People burned their furniture and cut down trees in the parks and in the forests which had formerly belonged to the Emperor.

When the blockade against Austria was lifted at the end of March 1919, people assumed that things would improve, but at first it made little difference. In April, a leading newspaper reported that Vienna had not even two days' supply of food, and the Allies, fearful of the spread of Bolshevism, informed the Austrian Government that no food at all would be allowed into the country in the event of riots.[16] Austria had exhausted all its reserves and had neither goods nor gold with which to pay for imports, so that it was dependent on Allied loans with which to pay for American food supplies.[17] The first of these credits had been agreed to on 5th March, but a long-term concept for ending the famine was not drawn up until 27th July, after General Smuts, in an appeal to the peoples of the USA and the British Empire, had warned:

> We witness the collapse of the whole political and economic fabric of Central and Eastern Europe. Unemployment, starvation, anarchy, war, disease and despair stalk through the land. Unless the victors can effectively extend a helping hand to the defeated and broken peoples, a large part of Europe is threatened with exhaustion and decay. Russia has already walked into the night, and the risk that the rest may follow is very grave, indeed...the effects of this disaster would not be confined to Central and Eastern Europe, for civilization is one body, and we are all members of one another.[18]

In April, Herbert Hoover, in his capacity as United States Food Administrator, extended to Austria the scheme by which the American Relief Administration (ARA) provided schoolchildren with one meal a day. In Germany, at Mr Hoover's request, a Quaker relief organisation, the American Friends Service Committee (AFSC), had been put in charge of the scheme; in Austria it was in the hands of one of Mr Hoover's associates in the Food Administration, Dr Alonzo E. Taylor. Within three weeks, 108,000 children were benefiting from the programme, but the mass of the population was excluded from these measures. As the ARA was not allowed to furnish loans to ex-enemy countries, a complicated system of payments had to be drawn up, by which the United States Treasury advanced money to the governments of England, France and Italy to pay for the food stuffs, and they in turn accepted notes of credit from Austria. Various American and European agencies also began collecting money for the relief of Austria, prominent among them being the Jewish Joint Distribution Committee, the Red Cross and the AFSC.[19]

The number of children being fed by the ARA gradually increased to 213,600.[20] However, the situation for the majority of the population still did not improve. Emergency shipments of food did little more than prevent actual starvation. An English doctor wrote of a home for old people that he visited where the diet consisted of tea without milk or sugar for breakfast, vegetable soup for lunch - then nothing more for the rest of the day.[21]

This was the situation when Hilda Clark returned to Vienna at the end of August 1919, this time in the company of two other Quakers, Maurice Rowntree and Helen Fox. Their first task was to find a suitable building in which to set up their headquarters. Even buildings were rationed, since the city was flooded with soldiers returning from the war and officials returning from the lands of the former Empire, which were now part of Poland or Italy, or had become independent countries, such as Hungary, Czechoslovakia and Yugoslavia. For thousands of these officials, the loss of the Empire meant that there was no longer any work for them to do. A third of the whole population of Austria was crammed into the city, which was often described as "a large head with a small body". In a city of two million inhabitants, half of the workforce was unemployed.[22]

Hilda Clark was soon offered rooms in a palatial building in the Singerstrasse in the centre of Vienna. The owners were glad to let them to an British relief mission, as they thought that the label on the door would provide a certain protection against squatters.[23] The rooms may have looked grand but, as autumn drew near, they became icily cold. The fuel shortage was still desperate. Although it was nearly a year since the armistice, no official provision for aid was to be made until Austria had accepted the terms of the peace treaty.

Francesca Wilson,[24] another Quaker relief worker, who had been helping to run a hospital in Serbia, stopped in Vienna to see what her friends were doing there. She was struck by the contrast between the beauty of the city, with its magnificent buildings and lovely surroundings, and the misery of its people. She wrote to her brother:

> Great buildings loomed out of the fog, and sometimes I emerged on a spacious boulevard or park, but all I was conscious of was heaviness and cold; everybody pale, everybody hungry, everybody silent and waiting. This is how a great empire ends, I thought. This is defeat - nothing dramatic, just hunger, hopelessness and cold. [25]

She and the other Friends did not want to take food from the starving population. At first, a minimum of food was given to them by the British army, often in the form of maggoty biscuits. Later they were supplied with tins and white bread by the British Food Commission, and, when possible, they bought vegetables to supplement this diet. As winter

Singerstrasse, showing No 16 on the left. (old postcard).

Second from Right seated: Hilda Clark, showing the effects of poor food and overwork c. 1920. The older girls in this Austrian children's home are learning hygiene in order to combat tuberculosis

(CLARK FAMILY ARCHIVE)

approached, the situation became almost unbearable, as they had neither coal nor wood to heat their palatial rooms and only one gas ring on which to cook what little they had.[26]

At first, Hilda Clark was too busy to notice the discomfort of her surroundings and the inadequacy of her diet. She had directed her attention immediately after her arrival towards improving the lot of the starving children, especially those under school age, who did not receive anything from the American Relief Administration. She saw very few of them on the streets, as most of the under-fives were so weak and stunted in growth that they were unable to walk. Many had developed rickets and other diseases as a result of malnutrition, and a large proportion was also tubercular. The hospitals, which had been among the finest in the world, were unable to function because of the serious shortage of linen, fuel, soap and food. The staff, too, were weak from lack of food. At one of the first hospitals the Quakers visited, the director told them that they had had nothing to eat for a fortnight except turnips. Conditions in the hospitals were so bad that most mothers preferred to keep their tubercular children at home, thus increasing the risk of spreading the infection to others in the family.

Edith Pye, herself on the verge of total exhaustion, and several of the men and women who had been with Hilda Clark in France came to Vienna to help, so that by the end of 1919 there were twelve British and American relief workers there, two thirds of whom were Quakers. Their first task was to survey the needs of 200,000 children by means of a medical examination. Only about 4% of the children were found to be properly nourished, whereas 50% were undernourished and 46% were seriously undernourished.

Hilda Clark immediately tried to arrange deals for obtaining food and coal from Austria's neighbours, the lands of the former Habsburg Empire, but she soon gave that up in the face of much reluctance, corruption and distrust. Even the Austrian farmers in the agricultural districts near Vienna refused to send meat or milk to the capital. First of all, they were suspicious of the Social Democrats, who controlled Vienna. Secondly, the amount of money they would have got for milk was so low that they fed the milk to the pigs rather than send it to the starving children in the capital. The government put high prices on what food there was but it had no currency to import grain, cattle or raw materials. Thirdly, because the value of the Austrian currency fluctuated widely, no-one was very interested in acquiring Austrian Kronen.[27]

Dr Clark sent urgent requests to England and the USA, begging for food, clothing and money. She was able to draw on the knowledge and experience that Quakers had acquired through working in similar crises

Three-year old Viennese children with rickets caused by undernourishment 1920.

in the nineteenth century in France, Eastern Europe and Turkey,[28] as well as on the support of the Quaker committee she had helped to found in London at the beginning of the war, the "War Victims Relief Committee". This was now merged with the "Emergency Committee" to form the "Friends Emergency and War Victims Relief Committee" (FE&WVRC). She convinced its members of the urgent necessity of saving, above all, the children of Vienna. "It should be considered", wrote Hilda Clark in her first report, "that every child in Vienna and every mother with young children is an invalid and needs special care and treatment".[29] There was an immediate response, and supplies of food and clothing began to pour in. Help also came from Quaker organisations in the USA, above all from the AFSC, which had been formed in 1917 to facilitate the administration of relief and was supported by the three largest groups of Friends in the USA.[30]

Next, she turned her attention to the state of the hospitals. In co-operation with representatives from several organisations, the Friends set about distributing the stores and medical supplies they received and tackling the diseases of scurvy, tuberculosis and rickets, all of which were prevalent. It was only during the first world war that the importance of vitamins for curing rickets had been discovered. Austrian doctors, who had been cut off from such research during the war, still thought it was an infectious disease like tuberculosis.³¹ Dr Clark convinced them of the importance of milk and cod liver oil in curing the disease, and managed to get both sent from America. The improvement in the first few babies to receive this treatment was dramatic.

There was, however, no question of getting enough fresh milk. Cows in Austria were down to a third of the pre-war number, and those that had survived were ill-fed and produced little milk, only two or three litres a day instead of fourteen. At first, Hilda Clark tried out an innovation, a scheme for producing soya milk by means of a process unknown until then. The experiment was carried out in a disused factory and was a success, but the scheme fell through because of technical problems. She then decided to purchase cows and foodstuffs for them, as the Friends had done in 1871, when they imported cows from Spain into the Loire Valley to provide milk for the undernourished children.³²

Dr Clark returned once more to Great Britain and persuaded the FE&WVRC to set up an Agricultural Department in the Friends' Mission in Vienna. She then got permission from the British Government under Lloyd George to export milk cows from Great Britain. Some cows were also purchased in Vorarlberg and Switzerland, but, when the farmers started to demand exorbitant prices, it was decided to buy the remainder of the cows needed in the Netherlands. Altogether, the Quakers purchased 255 cows and 6 bulls there. A small group of Friends set out to bring the cows back to Vienna. They were treated with enormous kindness by the Netherlands Government and received three of the bulls as presents to the Austrian people. The journey back to Vienna was enlivened by the birth of four calves.³³

Bernard Lawson, a former member of the Friends Ambulance Unit, who had applied to be sent to Vienna when he heard that the FE&WVRC was urgently in need of additional staff there, was sitting quietly one Sunday morning in the Friends Meeting when a cable was pushed into his hand and he read: "75 cows arriving this afternoon. Please make arrangements". His heart sank, as he had never before handled one cow let alone that number.

The Friends who had travelled with the cows were quite exhausted, as they had had to cross several borders during their journey, including those between the Federal Districts within Austria itself, with all the attendant formalities. When the group arrived in Vienna, it was to find that it was election day and therefore there was no one at the railway station to help them to unload the cows and get them to those farmers who had agreed to take them. However, by the time the Meeting was over, everything had been settled, and Bernard Lawson could breathe a sigh of relief.³⁴

Altogether the Quaker Agricultural Department imported 1,409 cows and bulls into Austria, thus providing the basis for healthy stocks in the future as well as meeting immediate needs. One of the pedigree bulls was named "Quaker" in honour of the donors. The farmers who received the cattle had to pledge themselves to send the milk to the hospitals and Infant Welfare Centres until the price of the cows had been covered. They also received nearly 3,000 tons of cattle food. Hens, ducks, Yorkshire pigs, Swiss goats and Italian rams were also imported and given to small hospitals, children's homes and land settlements.[35]

As the amount of work increased, more and more people were needed to supervise it and to carry out the distribution of clothes and food. Over a thousand Austrians volunteered to help the Friends with the distribution and received in return a small amount of food. Later, when the famine was at its height, this ration had to be discontinued, but they went on working without any recompense because by then they had realised the enormous value of the work. Schoolchildren also worked on packing the food into the right portions. At the twenty-one food depots, mothers with children under six queued to obtain their fortnightly rations: fat, sugar, cocoa, flour, condensed milk and soap.

The children were undersized and unnaturally well-behaved. They had pale peaky faces and black rims under their eyes.[36] Otherwise it was difficult to tell what was wrong just by looking at them. It was only when the mothers gave the ages of the children that it was possible to gauge how ill they were. Children who looked about a year old turned out to be three or four years old, but they could not walk because they were so stunted by rickets and general weakness. At one clinic, 100% of the nine-month-old babies were diagnosed as having rickets. Apart from rickets, many of the children were also suffering from tuberculosis and had to be separated from their families in order to prevent the spread of the disease. Because of all the shortages, from a total of 60,000 hospital beds, just over 3,000 were in use.[37] Supplies had to be found for the various hospitals, as well as money to pay for the cost of keeping the sick children either in one of the hospitals or in a convalescent home.

The huge cattle market, which had been built to hold 70,000 head of cattle but which was now empty, was taken over by the Quakers and used as a clothing warehouse and as a garage for the fleet of cars and vans which was gradually being built up for the transport of the goods which were flooding in.[38] Mothers of young children could buy clothes at a very low price. If they were destitute, they sometimes got them for nothing at all. Clothing distribution took place on a huge scale in two of the former reception rooms of the Hofburg, the former palace of the Emperors. As she watched the sad spectacle that took place there each day, Francesca Wilson could not help contrasting the scene with the magnificent events which must have taken place before the war, when the same rooms were filled with the most splendid aristocracy in Europe:

> If their ghosts had seen the long lined of shabby, tired men, women and children thronging the halls that had once been so august and brilliant and admitted to no one under the rank of count or baron, they might have been startled. For most of these people it was their first real shopping for years, the first time to see cloth made of wool instead of vegetable fibre or nettles, and shoes of leather instead of paper.[39]

The burden of organising all this relief work rested on the shoulders of Hilda Clark. As the number of helpers grew, so did the paper work and the negotiations with all of the authorities involved. Provision had to be made for the safe transport of goods across the numerous borders, reports had to be written to the sponsors in England and the USA, interviews with politicians and local government officials had to be arranged. In order to relieve her of some of these tasks, the number of people working in the office in the Singerstrasse was gradually increased, and one of Hilda Clark's sisters, Alice, joined the Friends in London to help in raising funds, selecting personnel for the work in Vienna, and purchasing supplies. She journeyed several times to Vienna to see for herself what was needed most.

A statement of accounts of the FE&WVRC for the year ending 30th September 1920 gives some idea of the sums involved. The total expenditure for that year came to just over £313,354 for Austria alone, not counting funds from other sources outside the Society of Friends. At the same time, substantial amounts were also being raised for similar work in France, Germany and Russia.[40] When one considers that, in England, £240 was thought to be adequate at that time to keep a family of four for one year, it is clear that collecting such amounts was a considerable achievement for a small religious society with about 20,000 members.[41] The favourable rate of exchange for the British pound, however, gave this money an immense buying power in Austria.

Funds came from many sources, not only from the FE&WVRC and the American Quakers. On 15th April 1919, a special meeting of the executive council of the "Fight the Famine Council" was held in London. This body had been founded largely through the efforts of two sisters, Dorothy and Eglantyne Jebb. Dorothy, another Quaker, had been to Vienna that Spring and seen for herself the slow starvation of the people there. She now moved that a special committee be appointed to consider the means of raising a relief fund for children. At first, she was Honorary Secretary of the Committee of this "Save the Children Fund" (SCF). Later, feeling that she was called to concentrate on the political side of the work, she handed the post over to her sister.

As Germany rather than Austria had always been considered the arch enemy, it was easier to collect money for the starving children of Vienna than for similar work being done in Germany.[42] Most people were surprised by the response to the appeal. Money poured in, the Miners' Trade Union alone collecting £10,000 within a few days of the first appeal. Nevertheless, Eglantyne felt that the Christian churches should be asked to make a special contribution, as the needs were immense. When she approached the Archbishop of Canterbury, Randall Davis, he refused her request that he should make a special appeal to the Church of England on behalf of the Save the Children Fund. Nothing daunted, she set off for Rome, with the socialist Doctor Hector Munro in tow, to broach the subject with the Pope. This time she had more success. The Pope promised to issue an encyclical, calling on all Catholic churches to collect money for the distressed children of Europe. Hearing of this, the Archbishop of Canterbury revised his decision, and on the Feast of the Holy Innocents, 28th December 1919, collections were made in Anglican parishes as well as in Catholic churches throughout the world. All the other denominations in England signed the appeal, so that it could with some truth be described as "a solemn call to the whole of Christendom".[43]

Hilda Clark's plan for importing cows into Austria filled Eglantyne Jebb with enthusiasm:

> Eglantyne's letters of this time are full of "Cows for Vienna", and she notes with relief that the Friends were sending workers to Croatia and Czechoslovakia to buy foodstuffs for them, only possible with the foreign currency which the SCF could supply. In the SCF accounts for the time, amongst the very large sums for Vienna, mainly handled by Friends, can be found "Cows for Vienna-£10,000".[44]

Another enthusiastic supporter was the British Military Representative in Vienna, Colonel Sir Thomas Cunninghame, who set up the "Vienna Emergency Committee" to collect money in England. He handed over most of the funds, which included his personal donation of 150,000 Kronen (6,000 pounds), to the Society of Friends to use as they thought best.[45] Altogether, this Committee collected more than 500,000 pounds before it stopped its work in July 1921.[46]

At the beginning of September 1919, the Manchester Guardian also opened a fund for the relief of distress in Europe, to be administered by the FE&WVRF, with a joint contribution of £500 from the proprietors of that paper and the Evening News. The British Government agreed to pay a pound for every pound collected, up to the limit of £200,000.[47] A. Ruth Fry writes that the sum of £98,381 was received by this means.[48]

Real generosity was shown by numerous donors, as a letter from Northfield Meeting in Birmingham to *The Friend* demonstrates. The Friends write:

> Owing to the extreme gravity of the situation in Central Europe, all unnecessary expenditure has become a matter of serious moral significance. Not that all such expenditure is definitely wrong, but it needs careful scrutiny, in the light of the terrible tragedy going on abroad. Our Friends on the Continent report that many thousands of children will die of starvation before harvest unless help is forthcoming in much larger amounts...Friends we know are already giving and have given largely, but have we definitely denied ourselves as much as we ought? Can we not each decide on some special expense we can forgo and devote the proceeds to this purpose?[49]

There was a continual drain on the funds of London Yearly Meeting.

Moreover, it was not only the children who were undernourished in Vienna. Roger Clark, visiting his sister in May 1920, wrote a letter home describing the condition of those who could not afford the black-market prices for meat and green vegetables. With his sister and another of the relief workers, Agnes Murray,[50] he visited a clinic for people suffering from *Osteo Malachia,*

> a disease almost unknown elsewhere, a softening of the bone with excessive pain due entirely to malnutrition and lack of green vegetables (vitamins). It appears to be confined to those with incomes under 10,000 Kronen per annum. If taken in time it is quickly cured with cod liver oil...If allowed to go on the bones actually break of themselves. The pain of going up (or still more down) stairs, of boarding a tram, is insupportable in bad cases.[51]

When industry in Austria began to revive a little, it became obvious that many of the professional classes and the vast numbers of state officials were more impoverished than the factory workers. And there were new groups of people, too. As well as many German-speaking people from the new "successor states" of Hungary, Czechoslovakia and Jugoslavia, there were about twenty thousand Jews who had fled from Poland, fearing the Cossacks who had sworn to free their Slavonic brothers of the "Jewish plague". In their long dark clothes, big hats and flowing beards, they were easily picked out and became targets of resentment, as they were felt to be using up the resources of the starving population.

There was also a quite different group of newcomers: the profiteers who descended on the city to make their fortunes at the expense of the desperate Viennese. One of the Quaker relief workers commented that the most painful phenomenon in the Vienna of this time was the tremendous outcrop of war profiteers, speculators and smugglers that had arisen from the ruin of the city. On the one side you had poverty and semi-starvation, and on the other greed, the wildest extravagance and luxury...These new privileged were everywhere in evidence. They filled the expensive hotels, swarmed up and down the Kärtnerstrasse, flaunted fur coats and jewels in the restaurants and cafes along the Ring. It was only they and the foreigners who could afford to go to concerts, theatres or the opera. Music and good acting, which before had been the bread of life to every educated Austrian, was the monopoly of this new class. Fortunes were made in a night. Sometimes the Austrian crown halved its value from one day to the next. Speculators who bought up foreign currency became millionaires without any effort of their own- they had only to have a flair for the right moment. The starvation and the misery of the city was enormously increased by these gangsters, for such they were. They held food stores and goods so as to force up their price artificially. They hovered over the dying city in those dark days like kites and vultures...[52]

She added that many of this "new bourgeoisie" were Jewish. Their behaviour intensified the anti-Semitism already prevalent among the impoverished middle classes.[53]

Many of those people who were dying of starvation were too proud to ask for charity. The Quakers sought some way of helping them which would restore their pride and independence. Many of them were talented amateur painters or skilled needlewomen, so the Friends provided materials to enable them to produce works of art, which were then offered for sale in Vienna itself, as well as in Britain and the USA. Francesca Wilson also opened a small shop in Gravesend to promote the sale of these products.

Meanwhile, the relief workers themselves were beginning to feel the effects of overwork and a poor diet. In February 1920, when the temperature fell well below zero, several of them became ill, and influenza spread rapidly among them. After a particularly bad attack, Hilda Clark herself was so weak that she could hardly climb the stairs to her office. She decided to go to a sanatorium in Kaltenleutgeben, a little village outside Vienna, to recuperate. There she had time to consider the fact that the relief programme was going to continue for a considerable length of time and that it would not be possible for the relief workers to sustain their efforts unless they were able to keep in good health. She planned to improve conditions for the workers by renting a house in Kaltenleutgeben, to which they could retire at the weekends to recover from the strain of their work. She also decided to provide canteen meals for them during the week in the Singerstrasse. Lodgings were to be hired away from the Centre so that, at least in their free time, the workers would no longer have to endure freezing temperatures.

Hilda Clark was beginning to realise that there were many people in Vienna who were rich enough to contribute towards the relief work. She also felt that it was demoralising for the Viennese to be completely dependent on foreign aid. To call attention to what needed to be done, she organised a *Kinderhilfswoche* (children's aid week) at the end of 1920. The Austrian newspapers and several organisations helped with the planning and implementation of the scheme. In this way, 7,000,000 Kronen were collected from Austrians and foreigners living in the city. Although those who were not so wealthy contributed as much as they could, Hilda Clark was not completely satisfied that all of the rich had responded as they ought to have done.[54] In spite of all her efforts, the money was still not enough to cover even a small proportion of the needs which still had to be met.

NOTES

[1] *The Friend* 13 March 1920.

[2] Hilda Clark's father, William Stephens Clark, married Helen, the eldest daughter of the Quaker Liberal politician and orator, John Bright, in 1866. Together they pursued many laudable aims, especially supporting the political enfranchisement of women and encouraging the fuller education of girls.

[3] Pye undated: 3

[4] *Christian Faith and Practice in the Experience of the Society of Friends* 1960: 108.

[5] ibid: 11.

[6] For a detailed account of Quaker relief work in France 1870-1875 see Sessions W. K. *They Chose the Star,* York: Sessions Book Trust, revised edition 1991.

[7] Greenwood 1975: 181.

[8] Hilda Clark to her mother, 16th August 1914: FHL.

[9] Hilda Clark to her mother, 9th October 1914: FHL.

[10] Pye undated: 28.
The hospital, known to the townspeople as the English hospital, was closed in 1998. It is planned to re-open it as a children's home.

[11] Hilda to Alice Clark, 4th December 1914: FHL.

[12] Sessions 1991: 76.

[13] Pye: 29.

[14] General Jan Christiaan Smuts (1870-1950), Prime Minister of South Africa, had known Hilda Clark's family since 1905, when he met her sister Margaret while she was working on the home industries scheme for Boer women and girls in South Africa. He renewed the acquaintance while he was in England during the war as a member of the War Cabinet. General Smuts was dismayed at the attitude towards Germany and Austria shown by his allies, and especially concerned about the reports reaching him of famine in Europe.

[15] Nicolson 1933: 282.

[16] In an interview with the *Neue Freie Presse* on 19th April 1919, a member of the British Food Commission threatened that any riots would be punished with starvation.

[17] Buxton 1919: 3ff.

[18] AFSC Bulletin No 32: 6.

[19] For a detailed description of these transactions see *Clark Family Archives, Street, Somerset* University Press 1943.

[20] Gildermeister 1945:71.

[21] Buxton 1919:10.

[22] Fry 1926: 193ff.

[23] *The Friend* 3 October 1919.

[24] Francesca M. Wilson (1888-1981) was a "birthright Quaker". She studied History at Newnham College, Cambridge and became a teacher in London. When she heard of the relief work being organized by Hilda Clark and Edmund Harvey in France during the war, she decided to leave her teaching post and applied to join them. She was at first refused by A. Ruth Fry, Hon. Sec. of the Friends Emergency Committee, who asked her: "What is your motive for wanting to leave it? Is it a genuine concern for Friends' work and the relief of the unfortunate, or only love of excitement?" By 1916, however, Friends' work had expanded so much that they agreed to send her to France, where she worked with Hilda Clark. In 1917 she went to work in Serbia. The book she wrote describing her experiences, *In the Margins of Chaos*, became a best-seller.

[25] Wilson 1944: 106.

[26] Pye: 49.

[27] Fry 1926: 193ff.

[28] For a detailed account of this work see Greenwood J. O. 1975.

[29] *The Friend* 5 September 1919.

[30] Hall 1938: 60ff.

[31] Wilson 1944:111.

[32] Sessions 1991: 56f.

[33] Fry 1925: 217.

[34] Lawson 1978: 11.

35 Fry 1926: 217ff.
36 Wilson 1944: 11.
37 Greenwood 1975: 226.
38 Anderson 1920: 7.
39 Wilson 1944: 123.
40 FE&WVRC Leaflet 83 *Statement of Account*s: FHL.
41 FE&WVRC Leaflet 84 *A Challenge: Is This Your Concern?*: FHL.
42 Horsenaill MS n.d.: 1.
43 Wilson 1967: 174ff.
44 ibid.
45 *Daily News* November 1919.
46 Carsten 1986: 43; *The Friend* 8 April 1921: 212.
47 *The Friend* 5th September 1919.
48 Fry 1926: 237.
49 *The Friend* 25th June 1920.
50 Agnes Murray, daughter of Gilbert and Lady Mary Murray, was sent to Vienna to supervise a scheme for helping old people, devised by her mother, who was a Quaker and later on one of the founders of OXFAM. It was supported by the *Manchester Guardian*. Agnes met her death in tragic circumstances while working in Austria (Greenwood 1976: 228).
51 Lovell 1970: 160.
52 Wilson 1944: 106.
53 See also Bauer 1923: 758. The Social Democratic leader, himself of Jewish origin, wrote that the middle classes "saw many Jews among the rich profiteers, they saw Jews among the leaders of the workers. Their two-fold hatred converged into anti-Semitism." (*Sie sahen viele Juden unter den reichgewordenen Schiebern, sie sahen Juden unter den Führern der Arbeiter. Ihr zweifacher Hass fand im Antisemitismus seine Vereinigung*).
54 Fry 1926: 236.

CHAPTER 2

A Quaint Assortment

BY THE SUMMER of 1920, living conditions for the relief workers in Vienna had improved beyond recognition. What life for the relief workers was like can be gleaned from the vivid descriptions in the letters of a young girl, Margaret Anderson, who arrived in Vienna on 7th August 1920. In England, she had heard a lecture given by Hilda Clark's friend, the suffragist and pacifist, Kathleen Courtney,[1] describing the dreadful results of the famine. As an impressionable young girl, Margaret fell under the spell of this remarkable speaker. She also seems to have welcomed the idea of a more adventurous life from the one she led at home. These two factors motivated her to volunteer to go to Vienna as Hilda Clark's secretary.

Even during her journey from England, she found herself plunged into all kinds of novel situations. In the course of dealing with visa problems, she managed to get herself separated from her travelling companions and was taken under the wing of a German gentleman, who proved so charming and helpful that all her prejudices against the "Fritzies" began to melt away:

> I came down from Passau second class with a charming (you won't like me saying that I know, but there is no adequate word) southern German. Fair, tall, well-made, I thought he must be English or Swedish, ripping manners, and before I knew where we were, we were discussing the whole of the War quite dispassionately like a couple of neutrals. We dined together and spent most of the journey talking...He said the Germans now fully accepted responsibility for the war, but he was very bitter about the way they'd all been gulled into thinking it was a war of self-defence on the part of Germany. He said the entire country was in the hands of the press, and the press in the hands of the Military autocracy, and there you are.[2]

During the journey they collected "a little following of other helpless people", two Oxford students, coming to a camp organised by the Student Christian Association, and a Swedish girl, who was going to work at the

Swedish Embassy, so that when they reached Vienna, the helpful German found himself with the task of getting them all to their various destinations, confirming Margaret's newly-won insight:

> So you don´t need to tell me the Germans are all bad, cruel, relentless creatures because I simply won't believe it.³

When she arrived at the "Mission", she was told that she was to have the temporary use of Hilda Clark's room in the Singerstrasse, as the latter was away on one of her innumerable fund-raising tours. They were no longer the bare, cold premises they had been at first. Instead, Margaret found herself quartered in a palatial flat, "all lovely white furniture. Then this morning my breakfast was brought to me - white bread, like the French bread, omelette, tea and ripe plums - in bed, by a nice little Austrian girl who looks after the flat"⁴.

As soon as she had recovered from her strenuous journey, Margaret set out with great curiosity to explore her surroundings. The palace had been turned into a kind of club, with a dining room and lounge as well as an office for the workers responsible for organising the relief work. Dinner, tea and supper were served there "so one only sleeps and breakfasts at one's flat". The quality of the food had obviously changed, too, and an Austrian family was employed to cook and serve it.

Margaret found her fellow workers to be a

> quaint assortment of English and American cranks of all descriptions - an extraordinary collection - they all have personalities, some of a distinctly Quaker persuasion, and others are adventurous spirits who've been through the strangest experiences in the Balkans and elsewhere. Quite unique...⁵

and she wondered how it was possible for such a motley crew to work together,

> pacifists, Mennonites (I haven't yet fathomed what they are), authors, rather smart young women from London; public school boys, strange short-haired females who tell you of the most startling adventures in Poland, Russia or the Balkans, as though describing a parish tea-party. I begin to feel I can never be surprised again. Some of them are simply splendid (the actual Friends, I mean) and have been through the most awful times in France, in spite of their disapproval running the same risks as combatants, one is forced to admire them.⁶

But she supposed that it was because they all had basically the same aims. At the beginning of her stay, she herself, coming from a comfortable middle-class background, found those workers with socialist sympathies the most irritating:

> I rather think I am getting rapidly cured of any socialist and pacifist views I may ever have had after two months living in this Mission. I would agree with them if they would only be broad in their sympathies and realise that many combatants were just as firm in their convictions as the Conscientious Objectors were in theirs, but they don't in the least. They will walk about showily without hats in low collars and red ties, thinking they are the only right people on the face of the earth. Don't for a moment think the above-described are the Quaker element; they (the Quakers) are quite different, gentle to the backbone and charming. I love to hear them "theeing" and "thouing", even the young ones, mixed up with all kinds of slang.[7]

Later Margaret Anderson's views were modified by her experiences in Vienna, so that a few months later she wrote to her mother defending the miners' strike in England and expressing views which she had obviously learned from her socialist friends. Many of the relief workers reported that the responsibilities they were given encouraged a different outlook on life and enabled them to broaden their sympathies and develop qualities of leadership which served them for the rest of their lives.[8]

That autumn, a large number of Americans came to the Vienna Centre, and the number of workers from abroad rose to sixty-seven, of whom only seven were Quakers.[9] Again they were a mixed bunch and afforded Margaret Anderson some amusement:

> I couldn't help laughing to myself and wondering what you'd all have thought if you had seen the quaint collection I was with! An American woman who writes, in the most awful clothes and a bit of corduroy velvet wound round her head like a cap and no hair showing. Very clever, I suppose, anyway she has an almost indecently high forehead with the hair brushed straight off, and she very seldom speaks. Then there was a New York merchant, a dear fatherly old thing who has come to work in our Trading department, and thirdly an American pastor who 's left his job and come here for a year to do relief work. I felt very English and old compared with them...[10]

On the whole, the American workers were much younger than their British counterparts and much less experienced. Hilda Clark was careful to ensure that they all worked on a voluntary basis but that they had enough maintenance money to keep them in good health. They were also allowed travelling expenses to go home on holiday after working for eight months.[11] In spite of great differences in the background, age and experience of the workers, most of them soon learned to work together without too much friction.

Their work was divided into various departments. As well as the Children's Welfare Department and the Agricultural Department, there was also a Clothing Department, a Trading Department, a section dealing with the problems of University students and professors, and one organising help for the impoverished middle-classes and for old people.

In the cattle market, the fleet of lorries, cars and vans had increased until there were ninety vehicles for moving the enormous quantities of relief goods that passed through the Quakers' hands. Many of the drivers had been conscientious objectors during the war and their right to work in England was still curtailed, so the Friends found work for them, either in the London depot or in Vienna. One of them, Edward Backhouse, had been a banker and had lost his business because of his pacifism. During the war, " he had to carry round bread for eighteen months in a London suburb".[12] Another, a former schoolmaster, was one of a group of conscientious objectors who had been sentenced to death for desertion in France in 1916. His sentence was later commuted to ten years hard labour, and he had been released from prison in April 1919.[13] For men who had suffered such harsh treatment and contempt during the war, the chance to do work which brought them the gratitude and admiration of the Viennese people must have been balm to their souls. Fifty Austrians worked with them, loading and unloading heavy sacks of tins, sugar and flour.

Part of the relief workers' time was spent in taking around people who came to see for themselves what was happening in Vienna, as there were reports in some English newspapers that the situation was not half as bad as it was pictured by the Quakers. Even Margaret Anderson thought at first that there was not so much difference between the conditions in Vienna and those in any other big European city.[14] To those visitors who did not penetrate beyond the large hotels, picturesque restaurants and fashionable shops in the city centre, it might really have seemed as if the Viennese lacked nothing, so that it became part of the education of the relief workers as well as of the visitors to make sure that they became aware of the misery behind the brave facade which the Viennese maintained.

Francesca Wilson describes escorting two sceptical hard-headed Scotsmen around the hospitals, depots and tenements where the sick and hungry were housed. The tour seemed to turn into a journey into the Underworld:

> Our pilgrimage through the buildings was one of the most gruesome experiences I have ever been subjected to. The car we drove up in had startled most of the inhabitants out of their dens and, walking through the courtyards, we began to be followed by children of all sizes and shapes and in every degree of squalor. The

number increased as in a nightmare. Gaunt women added themselves to the crowd until there were literally scores of people around us. The buildings seemed as endless as the circles of the Inferno, and when we at last emerged, we breathed deeply, thankful to have regained the Upper World.[15]

The Scotsmen had had enough and begged to be taken back to their hotel. Francesca Wilson felt she "had done her duty", as she had shown them more than enough to convince them that the need was real and far from exaggerated.

Another visitor, a cotton mill owner from Stockport, defied Hilda Clark to show him any real distress. In reply, she asked him whether he would like to have lunch with an impoverished member of the upper middle class, who happened to be helping at the Mission that day. When he agreed, the Viennese took him with her to the public kitchen where she lunched every day for 15 Kronen. However, having seen the lunch, which consisted of cabbage soup and potato stew, and the queue of white-faced, badly-shod men and women waiting to be served, the mill owner changed his mind and returned to his lodgings in the Hotel Bristol, where a room cost 5000 Kronen a night.[16]

Driven by hunger, many Viennese had started to grow their own vegetables and keep small animals on any available plot of land. By 1920, 70,000 families owned allotment gardens, covering 5,000 acres within the city boundaries. On such allotments they kept a total of about 240,000 rabbits, 300,000 poultry and 5,000 goats, much of this livestock being provided by the Friends.[17] Those who were without suitable housing built huts on these plots and stayed there, at least in the summer months.

Even before the war, housing had been a serious problem in Vienna. With its imposing public buildings, its palaces and churches, its parks and tree-lined avenues, the city was one of the most beautiful in the world, yet most of the population lived in appalling conditions, as the city had expanded too rapidly for the authorities to be able to keep up with the demand for living space.[18] At the end of the war, with the influx of new masses of people from the former Empire, coupled with unemployment and the lack of public funds, the situation rapidly worsened.

Quaker involvement with a new housing scheme began when several partly disabled soldiers approached Hilda Clark and asked her to help them to get permission from the Government to build their own houses on land that they had cleared on the edge of the Lainzer Tiergarten, a huge stretch of forest land within the city boundaries which had formerly been one of the Emperor's hunting grounds. Having nowhere to live when they returned from the war, they had squatted on the edge of the forest and now wanted to build small houses in place of the improvised shacks they and their families were living in. Each house would have a small plot of land attached to it so that the settlers would be able to keep hens, rabbits and goats, and grow their own vegetables and so ban the spectre of famine from their doors. Dr Clark managed to convince the authorities in the Vienna town council and some members of the Government of the advantages of the scheme, and once more she wrote to the Society of Friends in London, outlining the plan and praising it as one way to increase food production and restore to some of the desperate people a sense of pride in their own achievements. They readily gave it support, so that Dr Clark was able to offer the settlers money to begin building while they waited for the town authorities to work out the necessary legal procedures. Altogether nearly 12,000 pounds was collected to help the settlers whenever the work was held up for lack of funds, as often happened in such uncertain times.

Eventually, the Municipal Council agreed to construct the roads and sewers and provide water and light. The land was to remain in public ownership and the houses were to be built in a co-operative system, with each settler promising a certain number of hours. Lots were to be drawn for who should receive the first house to be completed.[19]

Gradually, the number of settlers involved in the scheme grew, until by 1926 three thousand one-family cottages had been built within Vienna itself and two thousand more in rural districts within a short distance of the city. Much of the building had been completed by unskilled labour, including that of women and children. Even the bricks used in construction were at first made by hand from sand, cinders and cement. Loans from the Town Council were often granted on condition that each settler guaranteed to give 1,000 hours of unpaid work to the settlement as a whole. As well as supporting the housing construction, Friends brought experts from England to advise on the planning of the settlements, drawing on their experience in planning "garden cities" like Letchworth and Welwyn. However, the Vienna experiment differed from the English one because it had grown out of demands from the people themselves. It was also interesting because it drew together people from all walks of life and gave them the opportunity to work together and take pride in the miniature "green cities" which grew up. Leading Austrian architects, such as Adolf Loos[20] and Grete Lihotsky,[21] also lent their expertise to the movement. Although it was estimated that the hand-made bricks would last for about twenty years, some of the houses still survive in almost their original form to this day and are aesthetically very pleasing. The name given to the first settlement was *Friedensstadt* (Peace Town).

The main difficulty the settlers had to cope with was that the value of the Austrian currency decreased enormously in the aftermath of the war, so that a house which cost 200,000 Kronen to build in 1921 cost

100,000,000 by the Spring of 1924. It was not a steady decrease but a state of flux, so that contracts quickly became worthless. The remarkable thing was that the spirit of co-operation and mutual help survived in spite of such difficulties:

> Confronted with such extraordinary difficulties, it was necessary to centralise the purchase of building materials and to co-ordinate the building Societies as much as possible. At the same time the various Settlement groups made co-operation and mutual service a *sine qua non* of membership. That the spirit of altruism should be the key note of an organisation owing its existence to the instinct of self-preservation is a remarkable fact, but still more remarkable is the fact that after three years of struggle, of development, and of ever growing success, the organisation has not destroyed that spirit but places the Movement far above any other of its kind in Europe today.[22]

Although the venture was in so many ways a success, it did not solve the housing problems quickly enough, so that the Town Council gradually turned to an alternative scheme by which huge blocks of flats, commonly referred to as "peoples' palaces", were built. They had several advantages from the Socialists' point of view. They were slightly cheaper because flats took up less ground and building plots were scarce within the city boundaries; they could be built near the workplaces of many of the occupants; they were erected along the main routes into the city, so that the existing infra-structure could be used rather than a new one having to be created; and lastly, and perhaps most important of all from the Socialists' point of view, they also included communal rooms and could be used to encourage a feeling of solidarity among the workers, while at the same time increasing the indebtedness of the working population to the Social Democratic party. The Settlements, on the other hand, aimed at bringing together a cross-section of the population with different educational and political backgrounds and helping them to bridge their differences, as well as enabling them to be largely self-sufficient as far as food was concerned.

The expansion in the number of tasks taken on by the Quakers and the increase in the number of workers needed to carry them out brought a new challenge. Dr Clark found that it was "one person's job to keep talking to the members of the Mission here without doing another thing, and that not to deal with difficulties but to make the most of their ideas. We've got a first-rate lot now".[23]

Luckily, she found someone after her own heart in Clement Biddle, a prominent American Quaker, who came to Vienna in the summer of 1920 to look into the possibility of bringing more workers from the AFSC to assist the British Friends. Like Hilda Clark, Biddle was interested in increasing the efficiency of the relief work and the services provided by the Quakers, and he was able to take some of the organising tasks from her shoulders. Through his involvement, more funds were made available from the USA, but it gradually became clear that Austria's recovery was going to take far longer than the Friends had anticipated and that even more money would be needed.

Conditions in the city were still very difficult. Life for many Austrians had changed completely as a result of the war and the break-up of the Empire, although the rosy picture Friends tended to paint of pre-war days did not recognise the fact that the lives of the workers in Vienna had always been hard. What was completely new was that now the professional and administrative classes were reduced to extreme poverty, too. Even those who had previously lived comfortably on their income from investments were now poor, as the Austrian currency was reduced to a minute fraction of its pre-war value. The exchange rate for one English pound was 58 Kronen in 1919; by January 1921 it was worth 2325 Kronen, and in September of the same year 9550 Kronen.[24] The effect on international trade was disastrous.

In his history of the Jews in Europe, James Parker tells the story of two brothers in Vienna, both wealthy: "One managed his fortune well and was reduced to penury; the other spent it on wine and luxuries, and continued to live in modest comfort on the sale of empty bottles".[25] Even if such stories can be regarded as myths, they do reflect the topsy-turvy world in which the middle classes found themselves. The old values of obedience, conformity and thrift must have seemed no longer valid, as those who tried to live by them starved, while profiteers and black-marketeers prospered.

The Friends in Austria had been hoping that the end of the famine in Vienna was in sight, but now it looked as if they would have to give continued support, if they did not wish to see all their efforts wasted. In December 1921, the executive body of the British Friends, Meeting for Sufferings, received a minute from the FE&WVRC with reference to the situation in Austria, in which it pointed out that the value of the Austrian currency had fallen once more and there were signs that there would be a return to famine conditions.

Alice Clark, Dr Hilda Clark's sister, who worked for the Austrian section of the FE&WVRC in London and who had just returned from a visit to Vienna, explained that the child feeding programme had had to be extended, and 30,000 children under four years of age were now being fed. More help would have to be given to the professional classes, university professors, students and all the "genteel" people who had to live on a fixed pension, as the value of State pensions had now dwindled to almost nothing. Usually these people were the ones who were too proud to ask for help and who had survived so far by selling anything of value that they possessed. However, the famine had gone on so long that they now had nothing left to sell.[26]

> The great problem of the coming months will be more and more that of the superfluous official, and of the many members of the middle class. To these Austria has owed her fame in the past. And if the world is not now ready to pay for their culture and contribution to knowledge, future generations, turning in more peaceful times to arts and science, will be thankful indeed to the people in England and America who are today trying to save this class from extinction [27]

Roger Clark described the breakfasts at the universities, provided from relief funds, where the students paid a small amount and in return got a breakfast, consisting of "a good cup of cocoa (1/4 litre) and a good large piece of bread, and, when they can, a bit of bully beef or a herring". Sometimes it was the only food they got that day. Roger Clark talked to one student, whose mother, a widow, with a pension of 624 Kronen per month, had three children to keep. He commented, "One thought the boy had no right to think of the University"[28]. Many students, however, went on with their studies, although they were too weak to concentrate properly, simply because there was no alternative. It was quite impossible for most of them to find employment.

Having listened to such reports, Meeting for Sufferings considered what ought to be done. They began to wonder whether they could sustain the continual drain on their funds much longer. One Friend thought that "there was a danger of funds sorely needed for our schools and other work at home being poured out to keep people alive in other countries, and of our taking part in an internationalism for which the Society of Friends had no real call".[29] Another pointed out that the feeding was only touching the surface: "The distress was one of the results arising out of the false ideas embodied in the Peace Treaties, which were based on the idea of punishing Austria and Germany. It was surely of primary importance to influence public opinion in favour of revising the treaty".[30] The "sense of the meeting" was, however, that the matter should be "earnestly commended to the attention and support of Friends".

Realising that British Friends could not be expected to find even greater sums of money, Hilda Clark decided to make a personal appeal to Quakers in the USA and travelled there in the autumn of 1921 to convince them of the necessity for continued support of the relief work. Raising adequate funds proved to be even more complicated than she had imagined. Accompanied by Edith Pye, she travelled to several Meetings, before going on to Philadelphia to consult the Executive Secretary of the AFSC, reporting to her sister on 31st October:

> We have now been here 21 days and have spoken at 27 meetings, 18 of which we both spoke at, and I have had 5 and Edie 4 separately...We got to Philadelphia midday Friday and had some talk with Wilbur K. Thomas. I do not think myself that he has the remotest idea how to raise money. He would like us to stay and do more definite money-raising, especially out West...but I really don't think it's my job..."[31]

The tour was very tiring and did not add as much to the funds as Hilda Clark had hoped, since, although the Friends were very generous in responding to her appeal, the AFSC had a different concept of how the funds should be allocated. The extra money was not ear-marked for relief in Austria but put into a common fund and then allocated according to whichever cause seemed the most deserving, and at that time it seemed to be Russia rather than Austria:

> Among Friends there is a tendency to leave the allocating to the AFSC and I don't know how much advantage Austria will get from any extra money we've encouraged them to give.[32]

The trip lasted two months, and Hilda Clark returned to Vienna, feeling tired and dispirited, having realised that there were great differences between the methods and aims of the Committees in London and the USA, even "a persistent sense of antagonism to the London Committee" on the part of some of the executives of the AFSC; "they cannot understand that there is any value in people of different ways of working learning to combine - they think you must always unite in one way - and of course that way must be theirs. I think this is the phase at which the Americans now are and that it will be very difficult to get round it".[33] She was glad that at least in Vienna the workers from the two countries had learned to work so well together.

Edith Pye attributed the success of the "Relief Mission" in Vienna largely to Hilda Clark's personality:

> Perhaps it was her simplicity and conviction that awoke an echo in those she sought to convince - certain it is that she was seldom refused. How well I remember the effect of her blowing in upon a group that was tired, perhaps dispirited with all the difficulties to be faced. Friend of everyone, helper and helped alike, in her presence a new life, a new sense of comradeship sprung into being. Difficulties caused by too close rubbing of shoulders melted away, and the vision, clear to her, became clearer to us all.[34]

Francesca Wilson writes with equal admiration:

> Hilda Clark had the kind of humility (for want of a better word) that had a liberating effect. I mean by that, that being intellectually honest, capable of self-criticism and devoid of personal ambition, she was able to appreciate other people's gifts. Great opportunity was given in Vienna to workers to show their initiative. Many of us had positions of great responsibility. She was not afraid of delegating authority and because of this, much more was achieved and the work often expanded in unexpected directions. Talents were used, not stifled by autocracy or entangled in a bureaucratic machine. Not all could appreciate her - she seemed to many aloof, to others absent-minded, but she had shrewd judgement, the vagueness was superficial.[35]

As Francesca Wilson says, not everyone was so enthusiastic. Margaret Anderson, continuing her character studies of the people at the Centre, wrote:

> I have got to know Dr Clark a little through working as her secretary, and I think she is a fine woman with great fire and initiative, but as usual with people with a very strong individuality, she is apt to be autocratic and the personnel of the Mission do not interest her like the planning out of the relief work. The socialist element of the Mission, consisting of the younger men and the less educated people, get up against her, and I have a cheerful time sticking up for Dr Clark, who I really do like and admire tremendously, and trying to justify her to the socialist element, who I also like very much. I see their point but it seems to me that their criticism is destructive...[36]

Some of the Friends in London, too, thought her far too independent and complained that she and her sister Alice often arranged things between them without consulting anyone else.[37] Nevertheless, there seems to have been no serious challenge to Hilda Clark's authority. The amount of responsibility the work entailed would have daunted a weaker character, and no doubt it was evident, even to her critics, that she had great gifts for organising and inspiring her co-workers so that they forgot their individual differences in working for a common aim.

Her family worried about her and sent repeated warnings that she should take care of her health. Naturally, she could not keep up the pace all the time. Whenever she could, she relaxed in the nearby mountains, skiing with her English friends. There are also numerous references to concerts in her letters. Once she even mentions going to two concerts on one day:

> I went to two concerts yesterday - a Philharmonic in the afternoon, when they played the Beethoven Fifth, as no one else can

- Weingartner is back from America. In the evening the Rose Quartet with clarinet, horn and contrabass from the Opera played a Beethoven Septet and a Schubert Octet, as I had never dreamed music could be, simply a revelation. We had extremely good seats, which also helps one to undiluted enjoyment.[38]

She also enjoyed the opportunity to listen to first-class opera:

> I am going to the Opera to-night. I didn't mean to get tempted this week, but it is the "Fliegendes Hollander" (*sic*) with a marvellous singer, and I have had such a wearing week, and it's short and won't be very tiring.[39]

It is clear from the mistakes she makes in her letters that, although she took regular lessons, Hilda Clark did not learn to speak German well. During working hours, she relied on an interpreter and an Austrian secretary. She spent most of her day either with the poor and needy, or with those members of the Austrian middle classes who could speak English and could help her, either by giving her money or by using their influence to remove bureaucratic obstacles.[40] Sometimes such acquaintances showed themselves to be real friends, as was the case with Gustav Scheu and his wife, Helene Scheu-Riess. The latter was a journalist and author who translated many Quaker texts into German and wrote accounts of the Friends' work for the main Austrian newspapers, thus giving them a lot of effective publicity, whereas her husband provided the Vienna Centre with free legal advice, an invaluable service in a country where there was so much red tape and innumerable legal hazards for the unwary.

Another Austrian with whom Hilda Clark seems to have had frequent contact was Sigmund Freud. She first visited him in his house in the Berggasse and then invited him to dinner in the Singerstrasse. Francesca Wilson gives a tantalising glimpse of the occasion:

> Once Freud came to dine at Singerstrasse, and Dr Clark invited me to meet him. I don't remember much of the conversation, though I recall that when Dr. Clark asked him about Jung he said, "the English like Jung better than me because Jung serves up the dishes cooked, which I serve raw".
>
> I was interested at the time in the New Education movement in Austria. This was to teach from life, rather than from books. Half the time children were not to be found at school - they were visiting mills or the market, or watching barges being loaded. I had seen a splendid Viking of a man helping the children to make lessons for themselves in composition, arithmetic, geography, history and drawing, out of these experiences, and had been much impressed, but Freud was sceptical. "In the old days", he said, "education at least knew what it was aiming at, but this movement was unplanned and rudderless - it had no defined purpose.

> In the hands of an incompetent teacher, this free education is worse than the old". "Education theory is in the melting pot", I said. "It always will be", he answered.
>
> Freud, I thought, was like one of Michael Angelo's statues of the Hebrew prophets. You could tell from his eyes that he saw farther and more deeply than ordinary human beings. There was tragedy as well as nobility in his face.[41]

While enjoying the company of a few friends who shared her interests, Hilda Clark obviously felt that purely social occasions, at which she had to mix with all kinds of people, were a great strain, as a letter dated 8th April 1922 illustrates:

> Yesterday was quite a good Mission Social - a musical evening, not one of the best we have had as regards music except for a very beautiful singer. There was a tiresome long recitation. People seemed to enjoy themselves and mixed well. They are always rather exhausting occasions though. This afternoon we went to an extra

Hilda Clark recuperating in Kaltenleutgeben
(CLARK FAMILY ARCHIVE)

Philharmonic. I have not been to any of the series this winter, having failed to get tickets. Weingartner was conducting a Brahms programme...absolutely wonderful.[42]

It seems clear that Hilda Clark did not feel much affinity with the Viennese people who came to the Sunday Meeting. She felt exasperated by their passivity and also by the lack of self-discipline they showed during the Meeting. By 1922 she was feeling "a little more hopeful" about it all, but just before she left Vienna in October, apparently in answer to some criticism that she had not emphasised the religious aspects of the work enough, she expressed her doubts about the wisdom of trying to use the relief work to stimulate interest in Quakerism as a religion:

> I think we must realise that the roots here are, as a matter of fact, not very closely bound up with the religious side of the Society as expressed in the Friends' Meeting. It may grow if it turns more that way. All I want to make sure is that we don't lose something we have had here, which I don't think is described by "merely ethical" – whatever that may mean. I think there has been a very deep-rooted determination in all the relief work to express religion in service – and I think there has been an extraordinary amount of transmission of the enthusiasm and principles involved in this.
>
> It is very imperfect, just as much of the expression of the religious side is imperfect - both often fail to convince others - but I believe both are needed, and where we fail to combine them we must do our best in whichever way we can express ourselves best.
>
> The influence of the Friends Relief Mission as an expression of disinterested service and practical brotherhood is quite a big thing and reaches many who are not reached by words alone.[43]

She did realise, however, that many of the people who had been working with the Friends wanted to keep up some kind of association with one another even after the relief work came to an end. In the summer of 1921, while she was resting for a day or two at Kaltenleutgeben, she wrote to her sister, Alice:

> I think we want a Friends Union of International Service to which all ex-workers in the Relief Missions might belong...we might enroll in it all the local people who have worked with us, who wish to.

She stressed that she was thinking of the many non-Friends who had been involved in the relief work, rather than a religious body. In a draft constitution drawn up at the end of August 1921, it was proposed that the members of the organisation should concern themselves with "education, hospitality for foreigners, visits to foreign countries, and propaganda for relief work".[44] Responsibility for future policy was, however, to be firmly in the hands of the members themselves.

In most of the European countries which took up the idea, the Friends International Service Union, (F.I.S.U.), as it came to be called, was relatively short-lived. As the relief workers withdrew, interest flagged. In Vienna, on the other hand, a capable Executive Committee, which included Hilda Clark's friend, Helene Scheu-Riess, was formed.[45] Under its enthusiastic leadership, the F.I.S.U. embarked on an ambitious programme of lectures and summer schools. A number of clubs were founded for children who had been sent to England during the famine, and a trained youth club leader, Christine Clement Brown, was brought from England to guide them.[46] At first, Friends had opposed the idea of taking the children from their families and sending them abroad, as they thought it was more sensible to provide food for the children at home. However, when the scheme went ahead anyway, they agreed to support the parents of the children and ensure that contact was maintained with the children throughout their absence. Some of the children went to Bournville, a model village adjoining George Cadbury's chocolate factory near Birmingham, and stayed with the villagers there for a whole year, a generous contribution towards their keep being provided by the chocolate manufacturer himself.

At one time, there were ten clubs in various parts of Vienna to help the children on their return. Later the clubs were amalgamated to form a Joint Club, which met in the Singerstrasse and survived until the annexation of Austria in 1938.[47]

Another club for young people, many of them students, was run by an Austrian Baroness, Friederike Appel, known to the young people as Riki Teller. It later took the name of Forum Club. The main aim of this club was to provide a calm meeting place for people of different races, religions, nationalities and political persuasions so that they could get to know one another and learn to listen to one another in a spirit of tolerance and understanding. International contacts were encouraged, and people from the club visited both England and America.[48] A hostel for foreign visitors was also established in the Singerstrasse. Many of the visitors who stayed there were persuaded to give talks on a variety of subjects during their stay in Vienna.

Compared with the vast sums of money which passed through the hands of other relief agencies, the amounts raised by the Friends were not huge, but the value of the work was increased tremendously by Hilda Clark's insistence that, once the emergency measures necessitated by the famine were no longer necessary, the long-term aim should be to restore Austrian pride and independence and leave something of value when the relief work came to an end. The help given to housing schemes, to hospitals and to the child welfare system, the replenishment of the depleted livestock and the organisation of clubs to enable Austrians with conflicting views to meet in a neutral place and to make international contacts, all these measures made a modest but valuable contribution towards stabilising the country as well as restoring confidence in its future.

Having initiated so many activities, Hilda Clark decided that the time had come for her to leave Vienna. In October 1922, she laid down responsibility for the relief work and departed as quietly as she had come. Her next task lay in Poland, where conditions were even more desperate than they were in Austria. However, she frequently returned to Vienna in times of crisis, for the city's troubles were by no means over.

NOTES

[1] For a description of Kathleen Courtney's background and career see: Haslem B. *From Suffrage to Internationalism: the Political Evolution of Three British Feminists 1908-1939*. New York Peter Lang 1999.
[2] Margaret Anderson to her mother 7th August 1920 *Private Letters* (copies in the possession of the writer).
[3] ibid.
[4] ibid.
[5] ibid.
[6] Margaret Anderson to her mother 11th August 1920.
[7] Margaret Anderson to her mother 23rd September 1920.
[8] For a discussion of the effects of relief work on the individual and on the Quaker Meetings in Britain and USA see Hall W. *Quaker International Work in Europe since 1914*. Geneva 1938.
[9] Greenwood 1978: 250.
[10] Margaret Anderson to her mother 19th September 1920.
[11] Hilda Clark to Kathleen Courtney 12 November 1921. Clark Archive/H. C. 6.
[12] Edward Backhouse lost his life in a tragic accident in the Alps in 1922.
[13] Fry 1926: 207.
[14] Margaret Anderson to her mother 9th August 1920.
[15] Pamphlet "A Day in Vienna" 1920: 9 (in the writer's possession).
[16] Margaret Anderson to her mother 1st May 1921.
[17] Fry 1926: 231.
[18] The city had grown from barely half a million in 1860 to more than two million by 1910. See Fassmann H. & Münz R 1995: 17.
[19] Atherton Smith A. 1926: 22ff.

20 Adolf Loos had been influenced by the simplicity and functionality of Shaker furniture in USA. His architecture aimed at a radical simplification, where every design was adapted to its own specific use. For a description of "functionalism" in Viennese architecture see: Janik A. & Toulmin S.: *Wittgenstein's Vienna* London: Weidenfeld & Nicolson 1973.
21 Grete Lihotsky followed similar principles to Loos in her architectural designs. She also designed the first "fitted kitchen" to make the best use of limited space.
22 Atherton Smith A. 1926: 4.
23 Clark n.d.: 58.
24 *The Friend* 21st October 1921.
25 Parker 1939: 132.
26 Leaflet 84 published by the FE&WVRC lists some of the salaries and disability pensions received at that time by the middle classes. A university professor earned between 20,000 and 37,000 Kronen a year, a primary school teacher between 15,000 and 18,000, whereas a totally disabled officer would get between 30,000 and 38,000 Kronen. The widow of an army officer received between 11,000 and 13,000, and other widows between 4,000 and 6,000 Kronen. How difficult it was to survive on such salaries becomes clear when one reads that the cost of providing a family of four with the most basic necessities, allowing nothing for clothing, was estimated at 120,000 Kronen a year.
27 *The Friend* 8th April 1921.
28 Lovell 1970: 159.
29 *The Friend* 9th December 1921.
30 Ibid.
31 Hilda Clark to Alice Clark 31 October 1921: Clark Archive/H. C. 6.
32 Hilda Clark to Alice Clark 12 November 1921: Clark Archive/H. C. 6.
33 Hilda Clark to Alice Clark: 17th October 1921:Clark Archive/H.C.6.
34 Clark n.d.: 16f.
35 Wilson 1944: 138.
36 Margaret Anderson to her mother 11th November 1921.
37 Greenwood 1978: 231.
38 Clark n.d.: 55.
39 Clark n.d.: 60.
40 In a letter dated July, 1919, she mentions a visit to "a delightful old gentleman named Ludwig Wittgenstein, who owns a number of estates in various parts of Austria and Moravia, and who lives in one in the Wiener Wald about fifty kilometres from here. There he has a fine herd of cows and has for many months supplied Dr Weiss's Infant Welfare Centres with 100 litres of milk daily...He expresses great shame at

Austria's crime in beginning the war, but he did not respond to our suggestion that we were also wrong in supporting the war system". This could hardly be the philosopher Wittgenstein, who was only thirty at the time. It was probably his uncle of the same name.

[41] Wilson 1944: 118.
[42] Clark n.d.: 70.
[43] Clark n.d.: 68.
[44] Greenwood 1978: 229.
[45] Horsenaill n.d.:2.1
[46] Brown 1934: 3ff.
[47] Greenwood 1978: 229.
[48] Jones 1937: 150.

CHAPTER 3

Prophetic Vision

TO UNDERSTAND the fervor with which the Society of Friends supported the relief work in Germany and Austria after the first world war, it is necessary to trace the developments in Quaker thinking from the outbreak of war in 1914. The war had come as a great shock and disappointment to all those Friends in Britain who had been working for many years in various peace organizations, especially when they realized that the main churches were not prepared to make any protest against it. In fact, the clergy were just as carried away by the engulfing war fever as were the majority of the middle classes:

> It was admittedly difficult to know what to do. A world war between Christian nations, justified on both sides by distinguished ministers of religion, must constitute an impossible moral dilemma for the more sensitive. The defence of Belgium seemed the soundest and simplest moral grounds for going to war, and not many could take the road of absolute pacifism.[1]

Even for the Society of Friends, the first few months after the beginning of the war were a time of uncertainty. Some of its members

> followed a course exactly contrary to usual Quaker practice - they tried to force official support of the War on the Society as a whole, and some even tried to act as interpreters of the Society they had already forsaken. It was further known that a number of Friends were active in recruiting, and in the manufacture of munitions, and that more than two hundred and fifty young men had enlisted in the Army or Navy or were engaged in other military pursuits.[2]

However, in May 1915, at the first Yearly Meeting held since the outbreak of war, a renewal of the Peace Testimony was minuted, which left no doubt of the Society's opposition to the war and expressed regret that it had not been "as effectively presented as it should have been". It called on Friends "to be more faithful and to meet fearlessly the unprecedented challenge of today".[3]

In the same year, conscription was introduced, "because the workers could not be persuaded to volunteer in adequate numbers, as their social betters had done".[4] Most of the 16,500 conscientious objectors who refused conscription were committed Christians, largely drawn from the Free Churches. Many of the Quaker conscientious objectors were linked to the Fellowship of Reconciliation, which had been founded in 1914, with a Quaker, Henry Hodgkin, as its first president. There were also 142 Friends among the fifteen hundred "absolute pacifists" who refused to accept a Home Office scheme requiring them to register for work of "national importance" as an alternative to military service, such as by joining the Friends Ambulance Unit. They felt that such work, too, meant aiding the war effort.

Among the conscientious objectors was Carl Heath, the full-time secretary of the National Peace Council, for whom the war had meant the total collapse of his dreams. At the outbreak of hostilities, the National Peace Council was disbanded, and his office in St Stephen's House, Westminster, became the headquarters of the work for "enemy aliens" stranded in Britain. In later years, Carl Heath said that he realized at that time that "the international peace movement, in so far as it rested on human wisdom, was built on sand".[5] He had had various contacts with Quakers before then but until war broke out, he had not been particularly interested in their philosophy. Now he drew nearer to them in his search for a new foundation for the peace movement and began to study the history and philosophy of Quakerism.[6]

He joined the Society of Friends in 1916, and at an unofficial meeting of Friends, the "Easter Settlement", held in Yorkshire in April 1917, he spoke for the first time of his vision for the future. He had come to see Quakers as being in a unique position to influence developments in Europe once the war was over because in its essence it was a creed which united people rather than dividing them. In order to further the cause of peace and understanding among nations, he proposed the setting up of "Quaker Embassies" in every European capital as soon as possible after the end of hostilities.

Considering that Friends usually proceed cautiously, testing new visions very carefully before acting on them, it is surprising how quickly Carl Heath, a relative newcomer to the Society and unknown to most of its members, managed to win support for this idea. Within two years the proposal had been accepted by both London and Dublin Yearly Meetings. This can be attributed partly to the strength of Carl Heath's conviction and to his eloquence, but perhaps it also reflects the need that many Friends felt for signs of hope after the disaster of war.[7]

Carl Heath wanted a new fusion of spiritual and social concerns, as he traced the ineffectuality of the Christian churches to the "departmentalisation" of the world into the spiritual and the material. This had replaced the early Christian concept of the Kingdom, which in his view had included the idea of striving towards a just social order and did not advocate a retreat from political problems.[8] He reminded Friends that, because they, too, had largely withdrawn from public affairs, the outbreak of the war in 1914 had caught them totally unprepared for the moral and spiritual catastrophe which had overwhelmed Europe. Nor had most of its members foreseen the full extent of the collapse of political systems, "the wreckage of trade and industrial stability, of civic liberties, of moral sensibility and spiritual faith", which followed as a consequence of the war. He stressed that the Society of Friends should no longer see itself as a religious sect, divorced from the needs of a wider community, but act rather as a "free, catholic, spiritual community, answering the cry of men in all nations".

To enable Friends to put these ideas into practice and to facilitate the setting up and running of the "Quaker Embassies", it was proposed that a new organization, the Council for International Service (C.I.S), should meet regularly at two-monthly intervals and invite American Friends to its meetings in order to make use of both British and American resources. The C.I.S. began work in 1918, with 140 members drawn from all the Quarterly Meetings in Great Britain.[9] Carl Heath became its Chairman in January 1920, with the prospect of also becoming its full-time Secretary, but as his appointment was not carried out in the customary Quaker manner, it was criticized by two "weighty" Quakers. Carl Heath had to seek re-election and was confirmed in the post in March 1920.[10] From then until his retirement in 1935 at the age of 65, he influenced the Society of Friends and encouraged it towards an involvement in Europe which, as was shown in the previous chapter, stretched its resources in both money and personnel to the absolute limit.

What strikes the modern reader as strange when reading Carl Heath's analysis of the situation during and after the war is that he invariably addresses his words to men and pleads for "universal brotherhood", without acknowledging that even before the war, Quaker women had been acutely aware of the necessity for taking political action in order to promote international co-operation and avert conflicts. When war became inevitable, they had denounced the lies and the hatred of the "enemy" inculcated by official propaganda and warned of further catastrophes in the future if the Allies insisted on imposing a crushing settlement on the Germans and Austrians. Many of them, including Edith Pye and Alice Clark, had supported the Women's International Congress at The Hague in June 1915, which had set out two aims:

1 To demand that international disputes shall in future be settled by some other means than war.

2 To claim that women should have a voice in the affairs of the nations.[11]

When their appeal for immediate cessation of hostilities failed, they continued to point out the futility of war. One of them, Marian Ellis, helped to draft the minute of the Meeting for Sufferings in January 1917, which expressed the conviction that Friends "must either stand for an unweaponed faith, the abolition of armies and navies, and reliance upon spiritual forces alone, or resign themselves to a still more complete organization of the world for war".

Thus, although Carl Heath referred to his ideas as a "new vision", there was not much that had not been said before. The difference was that he expressed himself more forcefully and at the right moment, when many Quakers had just been discharged from the Friends Ambulance Unit or had been released from prison, after having been sentenced for refusing to serve in the army, and they were looking for ways of mending the damage that war had been done.

In answer to the call for volunteers, several Friends travelled to Europe to look into the possibilities for "mission work", which did not mean proselytising but rather attempting to spread the Quaker philosophy with regard to peace, universal brotherhood and a new social order. Among those who felt in complete sympathy with Carl Heath's views were Maurice Rowntree[12] and Helen Fox,[13] who accompanied Hilda Clark to Vienna at the beginning of the relief work. They immediately started to explore the possibility of setting up a Quaker Embassy there, once the need for what Carl Heath referred to as the "temporary and abnormal service" of emergency relief work should die down.[14]

Hilda Clark herself was not very sympathetic towards their aim. Although she drew great strength from the silent Meeting, she saw the relief work as a priority, and she appealed to her fellow workers to

> put their backs into things for a few weeks...I think they will wish later they had done so, but no compulsion was suggested. Those who can justify it to their own consciences to eat the food and use the fuel needed by others without helping their material needs in such an emergency, must remember that if they are being maintained by the Committee, they must also justify it to the Committee.[15]

She explained her reluctance to exploit the situation the Quakers were in as providers of relief:

> I am very much impressed with how careful people doing relief work should be to remember that willy-nilly we are in a position of patrons, and have an unwholesome influence on the people we are trying to help- which we must not trade on. I believe we ought to be more careful to keep to a very simple spiritual message, and to be more careful than we are not to press our influence. I think this criticism that we are using the popularity of our relief to spread our views has more truth in it than those who make it realise and that all visitors from more fortunate countries tend to exert too much influence. One must be really pure in mind if one would really help.[16]

Helen Fox, however, believed that nations can recover from economic depression more quickly than from degradation of the spirit, and so she tried to concentrate on providing spiritual nourishment rather than food and clothing. She had a good knowledge of German and was able to communicate with the Austrians rather more easily than Dr. Clark. In various articles and letters, especially to her mentor, Carl Heath, she records talking to people from all walks of life. Writing to *The Friend* on 3rd October 1919, she describes two typical days in her life, soon after her arrival in Vienna. Her first job takes her to the garage of the War Office, (*Staatsamt für Heerwesen*), where she is soon surrounded by a group of admiring soldiers, who give her their views on the situation, which prompt her to wonder:

> What right have we to commandeer their cars, even for relief work, which they are too poor and too lacking in grit to undertake? We all feel that if we could only set them on their feet industrially, that would be far more worth doing than giving relief, but we feel so powerless.[17]

This mixture of sympathy and exasperation with the passivity of the Viennese is typical of the tone of many of her reports. A little later in the same article, she admits that it will not be an easy task to set up a "Quaker Embassy":

> One has all sorts of discouragements, and it is very difficult, almost impossible, to rouse the Austrians to take any initiative or even to make suggestions as to the kind of conference they would like to have. Work of this kind is rather in abeyance owing to all the trams having been stopped, but we always have a Sunday morning meeting and three or four strangers generally drop in. If we persevere with our meetings and extend a warm welcome to any to whom they may appeal, I feel sure that we shall in time get a nucleus of those who are really keen. It needs much thought and time.[18]

In another letter, Helen Fox describes a visit to one of the Infant Welfare Centres. Doktor Weiss, the head of the centres, talks to her in his broken English, which she tries to replicate in her letter, as it seems to her "part of the charm of his personality". The women who are queuing there are not the poorest, since they are able to pay a little for the food they receive for their children:

> Wonderful women these Viennese mothers! All through the war they have suffered through anxiety, bereavement, want, and, worst of all, the sight of their suffering children. And even now, when after nine months of so-called peace, things should have steadily improved, but have steadily got worse, even now they do not complain, but wait in a crowded passage with their beloved children for whom they have given themselves heroically, wait quietly and patiently until their turn comes. The standard of cleanliness even with the lack of soap and materials is extraordinarily high. "How patient the women are, Herr Doktor" "The patience of our women is wonderful", he replies, and adds significantly, "too much, too much".
>
> Ah! there lies the tragedy perhaps; a little more discontent, a little more vigour, a little more determination to co-operate, man with man, class with class, nation with nation, to lay the foundations of a new city, where want shall be no more.

Perhaps she realised how unrealistic her words were, for she adds:

> But one cannot expect this vigour and determination of the mind, when the body is weak and undernourished. [19]

Maurice Rowntree, who had been looking into the prospects of setting up Adult Schools on the model of the English ones, arranged for a series of weekly addresses to be given over a two-month period under the title "The Seeds of War in Modern Life". Helen Fox wrote that the lectures were well attended (20-25 people were present) and followed by a lively discussion. She herself spoke at an evening school on the conscientious objection movement in Britain.[20]

Maurice Rowntree returned to London and presented a report to Friends on the situation in Vienna at the Old Meeting House in Devonshire House. He gave details of the unemployment in Vienna - 180,00 unemployed from a total of 400,000 - and talked about the lack of food and coal. Relief work was going on longer than expected and still swallowing up enormous amounts of money, as well as absorbing the time and energy of those who would have preferred to concentrate on the "message work".[21]

In spite of the enormous difficulties, the "message" workers were encouraged by clear signs that there were people ready to listen to what they had to say. Many people held the Catholic Church largely responsible for the war and the subsequent misery of the people, so that the influence of the Catholic Church was much reduced. Tens of thousands were leaving the Church each year.[22] Pacifist organizations were springing up all over the city, including one called the *Tolstoybund*, which was an organisation of all those who had refused to fight during the war.[23].

Helen Fox made contact with many of these groups, as well as with the students who benefited from the breakfasts provided at the universities by the relief workers. She reported that some of the students were as much concerned about the loss of cultural identity as about material deprivation, and it was among these that Helen Fox hoped to find people who were genuinely interested in Quaker ideas:

> There are seekers in this great city, seekers of all classes and religions. There are those who have never belonged to any religious body, and many more who are impatient of ecclesiastical domination. Many of these seekers find their way to the Quakers, and are eager to learn more of this little band of men and women who, among other distributors of relief, are known throughout the city for their attempts to save the children from disease and death.[24]

Carl Heath wanted to look forward to the day when relief work would no longer be necessary:

> The relief work, please God, will come to an end. We do not yet see when, but it will come to an end – as relief. But on that basis, and through the chances that work has brought, there is a wider and more permanent service among nations, which, please God, will not come to an end...Essentially, the work is a ministry of reconciliation and of profound international importance.[25]

In his view, the Quaker centres existed to bring the message of reconciliation into the personal lives of a large number of people. He hoped to influence the corporate life of the various organizations through conferences and meetings, through Adult Schools, in various types of clubs and religious communities, in political and social gatherings, in other words, wherever "way opens for giving the message by word or deed".[26]

To discuss the implications of these aims, the C.I.S. arranged the first "All Friends Conference" in 1920. It was attended by more than a thousand Friends from all over the world, with a large American contingent of 350 representatives, including the Chairman of the AFSC, Rufus Jones. As a result of the consultations at this conference, many of those present began to envisage a world-wide Society of Friends, which would fulfil George Fox's vision of "a great people to be gathered".

Helen Fox, also present at the conference, warned that the task would need great patience and perseverance:

> The work of establishing Quaker embassies must of necessity be done very slowly and gradually, and we need not be discouraged if we feel we have not got very far. It takes a very long time for us to understand the point of view of the people we are working among. In Austria we want to aim at an Austrian Quakerism which shall grow up adapting itself to the needs of the time and the temperament of the people. We do not want to foist our ideas upon them.[27]

She felt that she had been in Vienna long enough to understand the Austrian temperament, which was "friendly, artistic and peace-loving", and that she could assess the needs of the people. She hoped that Quakerism would provide just the impetus that was required to help the Viennese to tackle their overwhelming difficulties in politics, industry and religion. However, she also warned against the danger of expecting too much of "this patient, tired people".

For the first time, concrete plans for encouraging the formation of a Viennese Society of Friends were mentioned. A Study Group in Vienna was already considering aspects of Quaker practice, as well as social questions, paid ministry, sacraments, education, and a variety of other subjects. Several Quaker pamphlets had been translated into German, although many of the group were able to read them in the original. The C.I.S. had already established a Foreign Membership Committee, through which Europeans could apply to become members of London Yearly Meeting.[28]

It seemed obvious that more workers would be needed in Vienna to put Carl Heath's vision into practice. Helen Fox wanted people who, like herself, were willing to stay in Vienna long enough to make it the center of their lives:

> The ideal form of service in Austria is for some Friends to go out to Vienna to live for a considerable time: to live, perhaps, not as members of an English mission, but as citizens of Vienna, pursuing their ordinary occupation as the Viennese are pursuing theirs, and giving their leisure time to Quaker activities, as Friends do at home, and as many Viennese will be willing to do in Vienna. Surely some Friends could be found to respond to such an appeal for permanent service?[29]

However, it proved more difficult than Helen Fox anticipated. She herself had managed to find work as a translator of children's books for Helene Scheu-Riess, but it was not so easy to find paid occupations for others who wished to stay. One of them, Anna M. Thomas, was praised warmly for her work in Vienna during a meeting of the C.I.S. in February 1921.[30] However, in a report to a joint meeting of the C.I.S. and the

FE&WVRC on 10th May of the same year, Carl Heath, while praising Anna Thomas once more, announces that she is "looking to leave soon" and appeals for a concerned Friend to go to Vienna to give Helen Fox support. This cry was to be repeated several times, until Helen Fox herself lost heart.

In the Spring of 1921 both Carl Heath and Rufus Jones, the Chairman of AFSC, paid a visit to Vienna to assess what was needed there. On 14th April, Carl Heath was met by Helen Fox and taken to the regular Sunday meeting of the newly founded Vienna Group in the Municipal Offices in a residential district of Vienna, called *Hietzing*, where there were about thirty people present. It was felt to be a good meeting:

> the speaking was all quite short, and for the most part there was a very living silence.[31]

On 18th April, Carl Heath gave a lecture to 400 people at the *Technische Hochschule* (College of Advanced Technology) on *Spiritual Self-help*, and two days later he was again in Hietzing, where he spoke on *The Quaker Message and the Present International Situation*. His eloquence made a vivid impression on the audience.[32]

Similarly, Rufus Jones gave a lecture to an audience of over three hundred, mostly professors and students. "I have never had a better meeting", he said, "They literally fell on my neck". On returning to the USA, he redoubled his efforts to find funds for the relief work in Europe and travelled the country, making persuasive speeches. Americans of German origin raised enough to feed 500,000 children a day in Germany and Austria, and the ARA was able to take over the feeding of some of the small children who had so far been in the care of the Quakers.[33]

Words of warning about the dangers of having too high expectations of the rapid growth of Quakerism came from several quarters. John Ormerod Greenwood quotes a Dr. Buerle of Stuttgart:

> All religious sects can increase their number even if they do not hold them, as people snatch at anything that might help them…All this has to be taken into account in estimating the reality of the demand for Quakerism.[34]

Joan Fry, a Quaker who spent many years in Germany, also warned that "there is a danger that one judges too much of the general thought from the rather special people with whom we naturally come in contact". The Quaker historian J. Ormerod Greenwood lists some of the reasons why the membership did not grow as quickly as expected:

> The experience of the small Quaker groups in Europe has always been that a minority are anxious for full membership, and a majority (for various reasons) hold back, though they are ready for a

less formal link. The reasons for hesitation are various (love of church, distrust of Quaker doctrine etc); he may dread the civil disabilities of being "konfessionslos" or the penalties for becoming a pacifist, or he may feel positively critical of the Anglo-Saxon forms of Quakerism, with its unconscious rituals and its testimonies which developed in Restoration England and nineteenth-century America, and are thus applied in different circumstances.[35]

The name "Embassy" came in for considerable criticism, as many Friends did not like its connotations. "Outposts" had been suggested as an alternative at a special "Outposts Conference" held in July 1918, but this was rejected as having military implications. Carl Heath defended the term "embassy" and said that "an embassy was a ...centre under a well-concerned person, the parent of the whole effort". H. G. Wood, the Director of Studies at the Quaker college, Woodbrooke, suggested that the "ambassadors" should be trained at Woodbrooke and outlined a comprehensive program of studies for them. Another Friend, Henry T. Hodgkin, asked how the workers were to be maintained, but there was no further discussion of the financial side of the project.[36]

In 1921, Hilda Clark asked that the term "Embassy" be abandoned, and Joan Mary Fry, who was working in Berlin, complained that she was teased about it and that people referred to her jokingly as "Her Excellency". Under such pressure, even Carl Heath had to give way and afterwards referred to "Quaker International Centres (now so-called)".[37]

In the summer of 1921, Dr Edward C. Steiner, who was not a Quaker, travelled to Vienna as the representative and publicity agent of the AFSC. On his return, he wrote an article for the *Friends Fellowship Papers,* the organ of the British Young Friends, in which he described his impressions of the "mission work" there:

> I have heard the matter of the future work of the Quakers in Central Europe discussed among the workers themselves, and there are two distinct and contrary opinions. Most of the American Friends believe that they came over for relief work, and that it was their only mission and that they should completely withdraw when the work which they came to do is finished. This opinion is held in various degrees, from those who are simply not interested in the larger aspect of this work, to others who are hostile to the idea of any kind of religious interpretation of the content of the mission.
>
> The English Quakers, as a rule, have interpreted their work not merely as a chance to bring relief, but also as an opportunity for bearing testimony to the truths which they believe, and their public meetings are conducted with skill and good taste, and have

made genuine contributions to the religious needs of the time. They have done this with genuine ardour and passion in the simplicity of their living and their devotion to the needy ones whom they came to serve.

I think it is the English Quakers who, on the whole, are in favor of remaining in Central Europe...In spite of human frailties which have manifested themselves in the relief work...the Quaker mission to Central Europe has had a profound religious significance. It has emphasised as nothing else has the futility of force and the constructive power of love.[38]

As the economy began to improve after 1922, many of the relief workers left. Those American workers who remained in Vienna turned their attention to the fight against tuberculosis, receiving a grant of $100,000 from the AFSC,[39] whereas the handful of British workers felt that now the need for relief work was over and they would at last be able to devote themselves wholeheartedly to Carl Heath's vision.

NOTES
[1] Hastings 1991:46.
[2] Hall 1938:51.
[3] London Yearly Meeting minutes 1915: 112-113.
[4] Hastings 1991: 19.
[5] Tritton n.d.: 14.
[6] Greenwood MS: 1580ff.
[7] Greenwood 1978: 200ff.
[8] For a summary of Carl Heath' s philosophy see the Swarthmore lecture, *Religion and Public Life* Woodbrooke Extension Committee, Birmingham 1922.
[9] *Religion and Public Life* Woodbrooke Extension Committee, Birmingham 1922.
[10] Greenwood M.S.:1613.
[11] For details of this conference and women's struggle to restore peace see: *England's Cassandras in World War One* by Sybil Oldfield in *This Working World: Women's Lives and Culture(s) in Britain 1914-1945* London: Taylor & Francis, 1994.
[12] Maurice Rowntree was a teacher at the Swarthmore Settlement in Leeds, a college for men and women who wanted to continue their education in evening classes. He served two terms of imprisonment as a conscientious objector during the First World War, and was imprisoned again in the Second World War although he was by then nearly sixty. His statement made at the Police Court in 1917 shows his character: "He thought he was called upon, with what effort and strength

he had, to work with a view to a different way of settling disputes altogether. In doing that, he felt it became of international importance, affecting every nation, and first of all his own. It seemed to him tremendously tragic that the great heroism, which he honoured with all his heart, was devoted to work for destruction. He felt it was the logical outcome of a system of life which was prevalent in every nation. He held in detestation the infamous actions of Germany. He wished them to be quite clear about that. But he thought that really war would never bring peace, except the peace of death." (quoted in: Hobhouse, Mrs Henry: *I appeal unto Caesar*, George Allen & Unwin, London 1919).

[13] Helen Fox was the daughter of Elizabeth and Richard Hingston Fox, a Quaker surgeon. Her grandfather, Charles Tyler, was the first editor of *The Friend*.
[14] *Friends Fellowship Papers* January 1922: 6.
[15] Clark n.d.: 52.
[16] ibid.: 52f.
[17] *The Friend* 3rd October 1919.
[18] ibid.
[19] *The Friend* 19th September 1919.
[20] *The Friend* 19th December 1919.
[21] *The Friend* 10th October 1919.
[22] Gruber 1991: 13ff.
[23] *The Friend* 19th December 1919.
[24] *The Friend* 28th October 1921.
[25] *All Friends Conference* 1920.
[26] ibid.
[27] ibid.
[28] *The Friend* 14th January 1919.
[29] ibid.
[30] *The Friend* 11th February 1921.
[31] *The Friend* 27th April 1921.
[32] Ibid.
[33] ibid.
[34] Greenwood M.S.n.d.:1693.
[35] ibid.: 1740.
[36] Greenwood MS.: 1612.
[37] Greenwood MS.: 1595.
[38] *Friends Fellowship Papers* July 1921:147f.
[39] Greenwood 1975:231.

CHAPTER 4

Quaker Faith in the "age of the buttonhole"

WHEN FRIENDS had gone to do relief work in France during the war, they had been asked by the authorities to sign a declaration that they would not use their position to proselytise. No such declaration had been required of them in Austria. Among the provisions of the peace treaty of St Germain was an article giving full freedom to all minorities, religious, national and racial. After the signing of the treaty, Baptist, Methodist and other preachers arrived to set up religious communities in Vienna.[1] Nevertheless, it was certainly prudent not to draw too much attention to any new religious group, as the Catholic church still exercised considerable authority and was not tolerant of these new "sects", believing them to be endangering the souls of those who were attracted to them.

The Catholic church was also opposed to the moderate and well-organized Social Democratic Party, which remained the leading party in the Viennese Municipal Council, even though it lost control of the Government after the general election in 1920. The Church authorities was suspicious of these left-wing reformers, many of whom were anti-clerical and suspected of working hand-in-glove with the Communists.

Describing his life as a student in Vienna after the first world war, the publisher George Weidenfeld calls it "the age of the buttonhole" because "wherever you walked in Vienna, you would instinctively look at each passer-by to see which emblem he wore on his lapel. The Social Democrats had one showing three arrows on a round enamel background, the Catholics a cross, the Nazis a swastika and the Zionists a Star of David. Clothes also indicated political allegiance. Catholics tended to wear rustic, alpine clothes with leather britches and a felt hat with a feather in it; Nazis could be recognised by their white stockings; Socialists wore neither hat nor tie and would place the shirt collar neatly over the jacket. In this way, it was very easy to divide society into 'us' and "them", and to recognise people immediately as 'friend' or 'enemy'".[2]

Christine Clement Brown, who came from England to organise the youth clubs for the F.I.S.U., describes the attitudes of the young people who came to the clubs

> to profess allegiance to the Church indicated political leaning, and politics in Austria were even then a fervid matter, absorbing the energies and often the idealism of youth...Religion, with them, was mostly understood as organisation and often a political organisation at that – while any concept of it as a life of the spirit demanding expression in social form tended to be foreign to their outlook.[3]

Vienna was divided into bitterly opposed factions, and in such a climate it was not easy to avoid getting involved in the disputes. However, Helen Fox was convinced that the corporate silence of the Quaker meeting would help to break down all barriers, whether they were of temperament or circumstance, language or race,[4] and she persisted in her efforts to spread the Quaker message of tolerance and mutual understanding. By the end of 1919, a group of between thirty and sixty people, most of them Austrians, had begun to attend the Sunday Meetings in the Singerstrasse. When vocal ministry was given, it was in either English or German, according to which language came most easily to the speaker.

From November onwards, mid-week discussions and informal talks were also held there. A variety of topics was covered, beginning with *The Seeds of War in Modern Life.*[5] Most of the discussions took place in German and gave the opportunity for personal contacts to be formed between the relief workers and those Viennese who were interested in the Quaker message of reconciliation and international co-operation.[6] To Helen Fox, the Austrians seemed to be a peace-loving people, who harboured no hostile feelings towards their former enemies. She continued to stress that Friends were not trying to persuade people to change their religious allegiance but that they wanted to help to those who were searching for new solutions to their problems:

> This is a time of stress in Central Europe. Men have overthrown their political despots, and are in a mood to distrust their social systems and their religious authorities. Our aim is not to lead any away from that form of thought which is helpful for them, but to bring a word of hope to those who are seeking a new solution for the complex riddle of their present lives.[7]

Adult school classes were started on the English model, using the "Adult School Handbook". One in German was held on Sunday morning, another in English on Sunday afternoon.

However, as many of the relief workers were uncomfortable about these developments, it was soon felt to be advisable to separate the relief work from the "mission work". Both the Adult school classes and the

Sunday Meeting moved into premises of their own. The Meeting was now held on Sunday mornings in the centre of the city in some rather gloomy rooms in the Neue Hofburg, a part of the Imperial Palace which had been completed shortly before the war. A library of Quaker literature in English and German was moved there, too. During the week, the rooms were used as store rooms and a distribution centre for the clothing sent from England and USA.

Another meeting was held in what had been the Emperor's summer palace, Schönbrunn. The huge tracts of rooms there were now under the control of the Municipal Council, which offered some of them to the Society of Friends for their Meeting. Others were used to house the central administrative office of the Socialist *Kinderfreunde* (Children's Association), under its executive secretary, Alois Jalkotzy. This organisation provided education and care for the children of workers, in order to prepare them for a better future. Later, a Children's Home and a school for training young child care workers were also housed in the palace,. The Friends made contact with the different organisations, and friendly relations between the *Kinderfreunde* and the Quakers were soon established. Some of the child care workers became interested in the ideas of Quakerism. The *Kinderfreunde* were anathema to the Catholic church, as it felt that the Church was now losing influence over the children who flocked to the many well-organised events put on by this organisation, many of which were deliberately planned to coincide with religious festivals.[8]

A leading figure in both Quaker Meetings was Professor Rudolf Böck,[9] who had come to the Quakers looking for help for an old lady of his acquaintance who was on the verge of starvation. He had first heard of the Society of Friends in his schooldays, forty years before, and had been deeply impressed by what he learned of Quaker principles. Disappointed with the Catholic Church for not speaking out against the war, he now took the opportunity to learn more about Quakers and began helping Helen Fox with the "message work". Although he was only fifty-five years old, ill health had forced him to retire, so that he had time to devote to his new task. His wife and thirteen-year old son, Rudi, accompanied him to the Sunday Meetings.

On 15th April 1920, he applied to the Foreign Membership Committee of the C.I.S. for membership,[10] stressing that he and his family wanted nothing from the Society of Friends except the opportunity to experience practical Christianity coupled with true humanity. A guest book belonging to the Böck family shows that, from 1920 onwards, a steady stream of foreign and Austrian Quakers came to his house, and their glowing testimonies to the hospitality they received there indicate that the Böck family quickly became the heart of the "Vienna Group", as the Viennese Quakers were often called to distinguish them from the foreign Quakers.

Soon Rudolf Böck was writing to Carl Heath every month, asking him for advice and keeping him informed of the progress of the "message work". In a letter dated 5th July 1920, he wrote that he was trying to encourage further contact between the Friends and the *Kinderfreunde* in Schönbrunn, where by this time there were 120 children in the Home, and 25 young people studying to be child care workers.[11] However, at the beginning of 1921, the conservative government closed down the Meeting in Schönbrunn under suspicion of "political propaganda". This heavy-handed action was probably meant as a warning to the Friends not to get too involved with the Socialists.

The Meeting in the Hofburg was allowed to continue and was soon filled to overflowing every Sunday. One of the rooms there served Rudolf Böck as an office, when it was not being used by the relief workers for the clothing distribution. He took over the organisation of the two Adult Schools, as well as of a series of lectures on Wednesdays. All were well attended, as Rudolf Böck had a large circle of acquaintances among the intellectuals and artists of the city, as well as among Socialist educationalists and students. Visiting Friends from abroad were often asked to give talks on Quakerism to various groups of students, settlement workers, evening classes, and young people's organisations.[12].

In 1920, the indefatigable Rudolf Böck planned to hold a summer school in the garden of his home in Mauer, a pleasant suburb of Vienna, but Hilda Clark protested when notices were printed in the name of the Society of Friends and distributed throughout the city, probably because she thought the relief work would be endangered if too much notice were drawn to the religious activities of the Vienna Group. Following her lead, none of the American and British relief workers gave support to the venture.[13]

In the same year, Rudolf Böck accompanied Helen Fox to the "All Friends' Conference" in London, where he made a speech in German on the achievements of the Socialists in Vienna, especially the *Kinderfreunde*, of which he was proud. He wanted to stress that the Viennese were not just waiting passively for other people to solve their problems. According to Helen Fox, his only criticism of the Quakers was that they were "not giving sufficient public expression of our message", which he considered to be "needed more than any other".[14] While at the conference, he made the acquaintance of a young Quaker called Headley Horsenaill, who had been a conscientious objector during the war and who felt that he would like to do work towards reconciliation in Germany. Rudolf Böck was so impressed by him that he asked Carl Heath to persuade him to come to Vienna instead.

Among the people who came to the English classes in the Hofburg was a boy in his teens, Hans Schindler, who became very enthusiastic about Quaker ideas and brought his father and many of his friends into contact with Friends. He, too, travelled to England to attend a Young Friends' Conference at Jordans and went back to Vienna, full of enthusiasm and determined to devote his spare time to the "firm establishment of the Friends' group".[15] In the summer of 1921, he felt hopeful about the future of the Vienna Group and reported:

> We now have a real organised Friends' Movement, or rather a Quaker community in Vienna. Our Friend, Carl Heath was, as you may know, in Vienna, and he gathered a group of English and Austrian Friends round him to discuss the possibility of carrying on the Friends' meeting after the Mission had left Vienna. A short time after he left our city, the Meeting Committee called together a number of Austrian Friends and, as Carl Heath puts it, the Friends' friends, to start the self-government of Vienna (Yearly) Meeting. We had a splendid time, and Helen Fox was asked to be Clerk, she having a thorough knowledge of "Friendly" things as well as of Austrian needs. I myself was asked to be assistant clerk. Helen Fox and I will do our best, or at least try to. I, personally, am very glad that we can "stand upon our own feet " now, though we shall depend upon English and Americans for spiritual as well as material help for a long time yet.[16]

A second Summer School was held, this time in the Vienna woods, taking as its topic "Land Settlement Movements". It was such a success that it was decided to make the Summer School a regular feature of Quaker activities in Austria. The topic chosen for 1922 was "Total Abstinence from Alcohol, Nicotine and other Poisons".

A Young Friends Group of about fifteen young people met regularly on Sundays, often with an extra re-union on Sunday afternoons at the house of Rudolf and Katharina Böck, which seemed more like the home of the group than the rooms in the Hofburg.[17]

Among all this activity, Helen Fox again sounded a word of warning and appealed for help. She confessed in a letter to Carl Heath that there were great difficulties between the relief workers and the Vienna Group, which "got the cold shoulder pretty badly". The young ones, especially Hans Schindler, felt very bitter about the way they were treated. The future of the "message work" hung in the balance.[18] A year later, she resigned from the Society of Friends and from the Foreign Membership Committee:

> During the last two or three years I have had the privilege of coming into touch with the Anthroposophist Movement, whose leader is Dr. Rudolf Steiner...Much though Quakerism has meant to me in the past, Anthroposophism, with the flood of light it brings on the things of the spirit, is a far greater reality and force. And therefore I do not feel it right to be a member of a Committee which exists to consider the question of Quaker membership.[19]

Thus, the person with the most experience and insight into the difficulties of the Vienna group moved on, leaving it to others to carry on with the task that had proved too much for her. Hans Schindler, who had written with such enthusiasm about establishing a Monthly Meeting and collecting money for the "meeting–house we are going to have one day",[20] also became discouraged when his ideas received little support from the relief workers. His attendance at meetings became sporadic. In 1926 he married Ellen Bellamy of Skipton and went to live in England, where he seems to have had no further contact with Quakers.[21]

When Hilda Clark announced her intention of leaving Vienna in October 1922, it was originally planned to pass the management of the International Centre on to a small committee under a deputy secretary, Jane Bell, who had been working for the Quakers in Berlin. She took up the post in September 1922. In the meantime, Carl Heath had approached Headley Horsenaill, who was working in Cologne, winding up the child feeding programme there, and suggested to him that he should set up a permanent centre in Vienna. After obtaining the approval of the Vienna Committee, Horsenaill agreed.

Arriving in Vienna in October 1922, he found the situation "somewhat more complicated" than in Germany, where both the American and British Friends took an interest in the local Meeting. There was considerable uncertainty about the future of the Vienna Centre. Earlier in 1922, the relief work had been reduced, and the number of workers cut down. The C.I.S was gradually taking over various departments from the FE&WVRC, which was wound up in 1923, but there was still insufficient funding and it was not clear whether the AFSC would continue with its support once the need for relief was over. British Friends were having difficulty in finding the right kind of volunteers for the new permanent work:

> Quaker personnel was not available for all these tasks – and the committee often accepted workers with quite other than Quaker or sometimes even pacifist background. In doing so, it was hoped that circles hitherto antagonistic to ex-enemy countries might, through personal contacts with former enemies, be brought to understand them better. There were as well conscientious

objectors on national rather than Quaker grounds, who had little interest in Friends' religious views.[22]

Headley Horsenaill attended the Sunday Meeting in the Neue Hofburg and found it "a poorly lit room, not particularly pleasant", filled with "thirty or more pale-faced and shabbily clothed people". However, he had great admiration for Rudolf Böck, "his ascetic, aquiline features, eager, large eyes and flowing beard reminding one of some Saint Hieronymus".[23] At the first Monthly Meeting that Headley Horsenaill attended, Rudolf Böck read out letters and epistles he had received as Clerk of the Meeting. After that, "the wider group started coming in for entertainment – readings by an Austrian poet from his works".[24]

By the summer of the following year, Headley Horsenaill was able to report that "the physical appearance of the group had much improved – colour had returned to their cheeks and most of them had smartened up considerably in appearance".[25] There were, however, other difficulties:

> On Austrian Committees - even quite official ones - there is a tendency for members to carry on most audible private conversations, but in the small Friends' group, this tendency was sometimes exaggerated to confusion...Possibly also the strain which all Austrians had undergone during the war and early postwar years had left its mark on the disordered nerves and ragged tempers. One learnt with time not to take all that was said and how it was said at its face value – and to ascribe much to the "Austrian temperament" which would otherwise have seemed most out of place in a Friends' group.[26]

As Horsenaill's arrival coincided with the stabilizing of the Austrian currency and the beginning of an improvement in the economic situation, it was possible to cut back still further on the relief work. Twenty foreign workers and forty-seven Austrian workers were retained. Not many of them were interested in the religious side of the work. In fact, "some who were practicing Catholics regarded it as heretical".[27]

Among those who were suspicious of the Quaker "message" were several of the Austrian voluntary workers who were helping to distribute the clothing in the Neue Hofburg. They were mostly impoverished Catholic aristocrats or middle-class women, many of whom were receiving assistance from the Society of Friends.[28] When they took up the work, they had not connected the Society of Friends with a religious sect. The phenomenon of foreigners coming to help with reconstruction work seems to have been accepted as inexplicable and left at that.[29]

At the end of 1922, these women started making difficulties about having to share the premises with the local Meeting. They complained to the official in charge of the premises that they did not like the association of their work with "sectarian propaganda".[30] Presumably, they were also suspicious of the young anti-clerical students, who formed the bulk of Rudolf Böck's following.

At any rate, the combination of "sectarian" and Socialist elements did not appeal to the Catholic voluntary helpers, and the Meeting was forced to move once more. On 11 December 1922, it was transferred to an older part of the palace and stayed there until 26th March 1924. The rooms in this part of the Hofburg belonged to the Women's International League, whose secretary, though a Catholic, was "a liberally minded lady of an old and well-known Austrian family", who sympathized with Quakers and sometimes attended meetings herself.[31] The new arrangement proved to be much more satisfactory. The two rooms used by the Friends were large and sunny, with beautiful furniture from the old palace, and tea-making facilities!

Writing to Carl Heath in March 1923, Jane Bell says:

> It was extremely nice to be able to retire into Rudolf Böck's little room - which adjoins the meeting room... I think the premises we have now are very suitable...I regret to say that I think Headley Horsenaill and myself are the only members of the mission who have a real interest and close touch with the group of Friends here.[32]

Two of the relief workers from the USA were Friends, sometimes attended Meetings, and were "broadly speaking interested in Friends". But the others understood very little about Quakerism and had no interest at all in the Viennese Group:

> I think without any doubt that they looked down on the little group of Friends here. Where the mission came up against the Friends, there was sometimes an antagonistic feeling which was very trying... One feels the difference here from Germany, where there were both English and American workers really concerned for the Friends' side of the work.[33]

However, Jane Bell thought that Headley Horsenaill was the right person to deal with the difficulties:

> Headley Horsenaill underestimates the value of his work out here. His position is one which requires a person with tact and consideration in the uniting of the groups here – and I have seen him meet and smooth down some difficult situations. He also is doing exceedingly well in the land settlement work. The little group of Friends here are decidedly progressive – I mean they do not intend to hide their light under a bushel – so that there is no need to have anyone here to do propaganda for the society.[34]

In 1924, he was joined by Emma Cadbury from the AFSC, who came to organise a scheme for combating tuberculosis in co-operation with the renowned Viennese specialist, Dr Pirquet. She was to remain as Joint Secretary of the International Center for fourteen years. Like most of the American Quakers who came to Vienna, she was intent on doing her work efficiently and helping to provide an environment where people of different religious and political persuasions could meet and learn from one another, but she was not interested in building up a group of Viennese Quakers. Her attitude to her work is well summarised in the words attributed to her by Headley Horsenaill:

We are not here to make Friends but to find friends.[35]

At first, she was handicapped by her lack of knowledge of German. In a letter to his cousin at Woodbrooke, a visitor from England, Redford Harris, describes attending Meeting during a visit to Vienna in 1925:

There were quite a lot of people at Meeting this morning - a Miss Cadbury (American) spoke in German and mixed up "schön" (*beautiful*) and "schon" (*already*) – I thought she had made a mistake and I mentioned it afterwards.[36]

Language problems continued to hamper the British Quakers in their "message work", too. Carl Heath had recognised this difficulty from the beginning and wrote in an article in the *Friends' Fellowship Papers* in January 1921:

To reach the souls of people, their own natural language is an essential acquisition.

An early Quaker convert in Germany, pointed out that purely linguistic skills were also not enough:

You don't really know our language, I don't mean the language etymologically, I mean the language at the very heart of the people.[37]

This cry was to be echoed many times in the following decades. Rudolf Böck and Headley Horsenaill suggested Esperanto as one way round the difficulty, one which would at least do away with some of the arguments about which language was to be preferred, but their proposal was not accepted. For her part, Emma Cadbury took the sensible step of employing an Austrian secretary, Käthe Neumayr, who remained with her until she left Vienna in October 1938.

By 1925, all of the International Centres except one were being run jointly by the C.I.S. and the AFSC, which had been reorganized on a permanent basis. There were still considerable differences between the attitudes of the British and American representatives. American Quakers saw their task as finished once the need for relief work was over and had little sympathy for the Utopian Socialism so prevalent among British Friends.[38] Carl Heath, on the other hand, was worried that "the great prophetic note was being lost in "minor activities". In a memorandum on the work of the C.I.S. in 1926, he wrote:

> We run a summer school here and a little hospital there, we develop a club for British wives in one town and for students in another, we carry on a depot for certain needy people in one city or an orphanage in another, we finance a leaflet in French or Italian, or a book in German or Arabic. And all of these things are excellent and need doing. But there is a danger that we may come to think that a series of somewhat unconnected philanthropic and humanitarian activities constitute the primary realities of an international Quaker service. I am persuaded that they do not.[39]

He was convinced that the greatest need of the modern age was not "for a little good here and a little good theory there, but for the concept and application of a new way of life right through".[40] To fulfill this need, the Society of Friends needed to concentrate on prophecy and teaching, placing special emphasis on the perennial questions of peace and reconciliation. He was troubled because the Society was not united in its concern for overseas work and because it was not producing a prophetic message for social change. Nor were there enough men and women willing to commit themselves to these aims.

No one took up the suggestion made by Jack Hoyland, head of the missionary training centre, Kingsmead, in Birmingham, that Woodbrooke should also provide courses for those volunteering for work overseas so that they could learn something beforehand not only of the language but also of the culture of the country to which they were being sent. He, too, regretted that there were so few Young Friend who were willing to offer themselves for service abroad:

> It is a paralysis following upon the war, and the present generation is growing up nerveless and able to do little more than discuss its own difficulties!

But he also commented that it was becoming more and more difficult to find funds for so much activity. Some of the British Quakers did realize, however, that it was not enough to leave European Friends to develop their own brand of Quakerism, and so it was decided to encourage several of the Viennese to spend some time at Woodbrooke and to train them in leadership for their Meetings at home.[41]

In spite of the many setbacks and difficulties, it did seem at first as if there were many Austrians who were interested in Quaker ideas. Many were disillusioned with those authorities that had represented tradition and security before the war. The Emperor and his advisors, who had led the people into disaster, had been supported by the Catholic Church, so that some people blamed it, too, for the disaster and no longer trusted it to provide spiritual and moral guidance in the changed environment. They looked to other cultures for inspiration, especially if they came into contact with a strong personality from one of those cultures at the right moment. Quakers from Britain and the USA seemed to offer a stability no longer found in the old Austrian institutions. The peace testimony of the Quakers and their demonstration through practical work that pacifism did not mean passivity made an immediate appeal to many of the war-weary Austrians.

However, this did not lead automatically to an interest in the spiritual dimensions of Quakerism. The liberal elements in the city of Vienna were traditionally anti-clerical and anti-religious, and it would have needed Friends with much patience and perseverance to change the prevalent attitude to religion. Coming from countries where there was a tradition of involvement on the part of members of the Free Churches in measures leading to educational, scientific and commercial progress, the foreign Quakers, on the whole, do not seem to have made allowances for the fact that, in Austria, it was difficult to be both a radical reformer of the political and economic system and at the same time religious.

By not treating the Austrians as equals, the majority of the relief workers also seem to have missed the opportunity for building up the trust and loyalty of those who did show an interest in Quakerism. The gap between the foreign workers, living in relative luxury and supported by the safety net of their home communities, and the poverty-stricken Austrians was too great. Those of the relief workers who were Quakers - and there were not so many of them - provided the Austrians with instructions on the theory and practice of Quakerism, but many of them had reservations about encouraging them to become "real" Quakers. The Austrians were often suspected of pretending to be interested in Quakerism mainly for the material benefits they hoped to gain. While this was undoubtedly true of some of them, many of the genuine seekers were offended by the lack of enthusiasm they met with and soon drifted away.

NOTES
[1] Friends Fellowship Papers 1921.
[2] Weidenfeld 1995: 33f.
[3] Brown.1934: 7.
[4] Fox n.d.: 4.
[5] *The Friend.* 19th December 1919.
[6] Fox n.d.: 2f.

[7] ibid.: 6f.
[8] Speiser 1979: 71ff.
[9] In Austria, titles are important. The title "professor" may indicate that its holder is a university professor. More often it indicates that he/she is a grammar school teacher or has received the title for some public service. Professor Böck had taught art at a grammar school and lectured on landscape gardening at an agricultural college.
[10] *Foreign Membership Papers:* Box 1. FHL.
[11] ibid.
[12] *The Friend* 28th October 1921.
[13] Greenwood 1978: 251.
[14] Letter to Carl Heath, *Foreign Membership Papers* Box 1 FHL.
[15] *Friends' Fellowship Papers*: 1921 FHL.
[16] ibid.
[17] Greenwood 1978: 253.
[18] Greenwood M.S.: 1675.
[19] Friends Membership Papers: Box 2 FHL.
[20] *The Friend* 19th August 1921.
[21] Greenwood 1978.
[22] Horsenaill n.d.: 11.
[23] Horsenaill n.d.: 83.
[24] Horsenaill n.d.: 87.
[25] ibid: 84.
[26] ibid: 97.
[27] Horsenaill n.d. 33.
[28] ibid: 35.
[29] Friends' Quarterly Examiner 1923: 324. Woodbrooke Library.
[30] Horsenaill n.d.: 94.
[31] Horsenaill n.d.: 95.
[32] Foreign Membership Papers: Box 2. FHL.
[33] ibid.
[34] Ibid.
[35] Horsenaill n.d.: 97.
[36] Alexander File 1. Woodbrooke Library.
[37] Greenwood M.S.:1646.
[38] Greenwood M.S.: 1604.
[39] Greenwood M.S.:1719.
[40] Ibid.
[41] Greenwood M.S.: 1651.

CHAPTER 5

A New Jerusalem?

QUAKER WORK in Vienna in the 1920s is well documented because British and American Friends kept up a regular stream of letters and articles, describing their experiences to those who supported them in their Meetings at home. Many were printed in Quaker journals and preserved for posterity in Quaker archives. It is more difficult to reconstruct the story from the Austrian point of view because most of the written documents from the Vienna Group were lost in the various upheavals which are described in the following chapters, culminating in the closing of the Vienna Centre in 1942. In the few reports which have survived, the Friends' custom of referring to people without giving their names sometimes makes identification very difficult. Nevertheless, it is possible to pick out one or two individual voices and hear something of their story.

From 1920 onwards, numerous Austrians wrote to the Foreign Membership Committee of the C. I. S., applying to become members of the Society of Friends. According to Hans Schindler, the small group of Austrian Friends had attained an "unshakeable inward and outward calmness", while all around them people were being "tossed about", and Vienna was filled with feverish excitement:

> A postal strike is paralyzing public life; State officials are dismissed by thousands; hospitals are on strike; all sorts and conditions of men make their "walks" upon the beautiful Ring Strasse to show their pleasure or displeasure about this or the other thing; there is the Monarchist question, the Unemployment question, the Jewish question, even the Ruhr question, and tons of other "questions" - and all these manifold and exciting phenomena, birth throes of a new era in Austria and Central Europe, have stirred up our public ocean so that it is one heavily rolling mass of yeasty and turbid waves.[1]

In his youthful enthusiasm, he envisaged the day when all this confusion would come to an end, and, through Quaker influence, "the new Jerusalem in the Alpine dales, forests, meadows and towns of Austria" would be established. There is no mention here of the tensions that had already manifested themselves within the Vienna Group nor of the disappointment that Hans Schindler himself felt because there was little support from foreign Friends for his plans for building a meeting house in Vienna.[2]

By the time Headley Horsenaill reached Vienna in 1922, there were about twenty-two Austrians who were technically members of the Society of Friends,[3] with an additional fifty people who regularly attended meetings. Deciding which of the new applicants should be recommended for membership of the Society was not always an easy task. Perhaps the difficulties can best be illustrated by describing some of the cases that occupied the Committee, sometimes for months on end.

One of them, Willi Schubert, was conscripted during the war as a boy of seventeen and survived two years of fighting on the Italian front. Afterwards, he returned to Vienna to continue his studies and found his family on the verge of starvation, with his father struggling to feed five children, the youngest of which was a new-born baby. For the rest of his short life, Willi was to be haunted by the horrors he had experienced in the trenches. He saw war as the greatest of all evils, and he devoted his energies to supporting the peace movement.[4]

His first encounter with Quakers was purely accidental. While travelling back to Vienna by train, he listened to two English ladies talking but was too shy to address them. When they left the train, one of them dropped a shawl. A year or so later, Willi saw the same lady in the street in Vienna. This time he spoke to her and told her he had picked up her shawl and wanted to return it. As a result of this chance acquaintance with an English Quaker, Willi became interested in Quaker ideas and was especially drawn to the peace testimony. In 1922, he was enabled to spend two terms at Woodbrooke, the Quaker study centre in Birmingham.

The other students there did not know what to make of this strange young man, who, "when he came to Woodbrooke, seemed almost too sad to laugh".[5] How could they understand someone whose life had been so different from their own? Even the relative simplicity of life at Woodbrooke must have been a far cry from the misery of conditions in Vienna, where just to stay alive was a struggle. However, by the end of his two terms there, he had obviously learned to laugh again, as the entry in Woodbrooke's "Logbook" for 1922 shows. The students were encouraged to write about their experiences at the college, and Willi wrote a very funny piece describing his difficulties in keeping appointments. Nevertheless, as Horace Alexander, his tutor at Woodbrooke, observed, he still "had great difficulty in achieving equanimity".[6]

He returned to Vienna, feeling that he was going back to prison. Luckily, Horace Alexander took a special interest in him and went to visit him in Vienna. Realizing that there was some estrangement between him and his former pupil, he wrote on his return home, asking what was wrong. Willi replied that his tutor's visit had made him feel "courageless" (the German "*mutlos*", which means discouraged or lacking in confidence):

> And to tell you the truth, I even reproached you for being so "English" and so on... I thought you are just like the others, who think it is all right if they have not to eat on a broken plate and do not see people going in rags and do not see tears, but just the smiling surface in Austria. And they think that, so long as one does not commit suicide, then it is going quite well. Even in the worst days in Vienna, everyone <u>enjoyed</u> Vienna, and the people went like children through our town, because we never showed our misery...it is so difficult for most people to look behind the curtains and see what is behind the stage.[7]

This letter conveys the sense of injustice which many of the students in Vienna felt at this time because they had been reduced by the war to the state of beggars. The humiliation they had to bear made many of them susceptible to any radical propaganda which promised to give them work and restore their pride. It is, perhaps, not surprising that later on many of the most fervent National Socialists came from the ranks of those who had been students in the 1920s.

Encouraged by Horace Alexander, Willi Schubert wrote a letter to Carl Heath at the C.I.S., applying for membership of the Society of Friends, although this was opposed by the local Meeting in Vienna because Willi refused to give up membership of his father's church:

> A small group of Viennese had begun to met on Sundays, week by week, and Willi met with them and liked them as human beings. But their background was either agnostic or Jewish. Willi's father and family belonged to the small Catholic Apostolic Church (Irvingite), and for Willi it was too narrow and intolerant. It did not seem to him to represent the Christianity of Jesus Christ... But the Viennese wanted him to declare himself "*konfessionslos*" (without any religious affiliation). This he could not do.[8]

The Foreign Membership Committee of the C.I.S. admitted Willi Schubert to membership on 31st December 1923, although it had minuted on 1st October that "we wish to consider each case on its merits, paying special attention to any opinion expressed by the local group".[9] Giving their reasons for overruling the local committee, the Committee referred to another minute of 31st October 1921, which read:

> We think that formal resignation of membership should not be demanded of applicants for membership of the Society of Friends,

but that such resignation should come naturally as they feel the need.

In Germany, especially in the Protestant areas, dual membership does not seem to have posed many difficulties, but in Austria, because of the widespread political and religious enmities, such questions caused serious problems. Moreover, any Austrian who resigned membership of a recognized church and became a member of the Society of Friends, had to make a formal declaration to the State that he or she had no religion, since Quakerism was not officially recognized. This procedure brought with it several disadvantages, especially when it came to finding employment, so that many people were loath to take the step. Those who did sacrifice material advantages in this way in order to become Members of the Society of Friends felt, quite naturally, that others should be called upon to do the same, although some uneasiness remained about the fact that the only official category open to them, that of "*konfessionslos*" (of no religious persuasion) did not represent the truth. To this day, no fully satisfactory solution to this dilemma has been found.

The Foreign Membership Committee was not very happy about having overridden the decisions of the local group, and obviously it was a question which continued to occupy it; a letter signed by Carl Heath in April 1924 records that "the plan for admitting members is only a temporary one":

> As soon as there has come into being a local group of men and women in union with the great body of Friends throughout the world...it will no longer be reasonable or necessary that membership should be obtained through joining an English or other foreign Group. The Membership should be of their own Group and through that group of the Society at large. We call you, not to conformity to rules, but to a living, growing fellowship, in which we believe you will be led to use the best means for the strength and increase of your membership.

The local group might, perhaps, be forgiven for asking who was going to decide when that day had come.

Willi Schubert did not remain a member of the Vienna Group for very long. After he had finished his studies of law, he got a post with the League of Nations and joined the Geneva Meeting. Two years later, in 1930, he caught an infection from swimming in the Danube, and within three weeks he was dead.[10]

Another student, Herbert Schmidt, also had trouble with the local group about not resigning his membership of another church. He was accepted as a member on 30 June 1920, but resigned on 1st September 1923. The Austrian Friends seem to have issued him with an ultimatum, requiring him to decide whether to give up membership of the Lutheran Church or leave the Society. Headley Horsenaill wrote to the Committee in London twice in that year about why the Austrian Friends did not accept Herbert Schmidt as a member, explaining that

> the Friends' Group here takes a pretty definite position that those who wish to become members of the Society should sever their legal connection with another religious body. The Group welcomes those who feel fellowship with it as attenders at its meetings, including its ordinary business ones, and there are several who have attended for years in this way, but it feels that, if they have a desire to become certificated members of the Society, they should be willing to forego their legal membership of another religious body, with whatever privileges this may involve. This was not understood by Roman Zimmerl when he joined the Society, in fact he says that English Friends who were here at the time told him he could continue a member of the Catholic Church. [11]

For once, Hilda Clark found herself in agreement with the Vienna Group and wrote to Carl Heath, pointing out that Herbert Schmidt, like some of the other applicants, did not seem to have much knowledge of Quakerism:

> Does he really know much about Friends or their beliefs? Has he read any of our books?...We have seen several attractive people who joined Friends and then left us after a while. Such an experience is not good for them nor for the Society.[12]

The other Austrian mentioned in Headley Horsenaill's letter, Roman Zimmerl, had been working as a waiter in London when war broke out and had got to know Quakers during his internment there. In his application for membership for himself and his wife, dated 31st December 1919, he had clearly stated that he was a Roman Catholic "which cannot find consolation in the r.c. church (*sic*)". His wife belonged to the Lutheran Church, and of his children, one was a Catholic and another a Protestant, according to their legal registration, while a third was the first "birthright Quaker" in Vienna, having been born there in 1920 and given the name of North Gillett after the English Quaker, Rowntree Gillett, whom Roman Zimmerl refers to as the baby's "godfather in Spirit".[13]

His application for Membership had been supported by Edward Backhouse, who lost his life in an accident in the Alps at the end of August 1922, so that it was not possible for the Committee to confirm Roman Zimmerl's claim that he had been told that there was no need for him to give up his membership of the Catholic Church, but it seems likely that Edward Backhouse had not understood the complexities of the issue. Roman Zimmerl promised that he would take immediate steps to leave the Church, but instead, he borrowed money from the Quakers to go to Brazil as guide to a party of emigrants, taking his family with him, and disappeared from the records.

Rudolf Böck's only son, who was always referred to as Rudi to distinguish him from his father, wrote on his fourteenth birthday, the age at which children were allowed by Austrian law to choose their own religion, asking in his childish way to be admitted to the Society:

> I am today fourteen years old. So I come to you, asking would you like that I can become Quaker? I'll try in my life that I become a good Quaker.[14]

Another of the early applicants, Frau Bayer, did give up her membership of the Catholic Church, but in 1927 she decided that she wanted to return to the Church, not because she was disappointed with the Society of Friends but because she felt isolated from her family. Mothers were expected to accompany their children to the many rites and festivals which played an important part in Austrian religious life, and Frau Bayer's exclusion from them formed a barrier between her and her children. Her application was unusual, since the other women who were admitted into the Society at the time seem to have joined the Society in the wake of a male relative, husband, brother or father, and give no indication of their own opinions. This does not necessarily mean that they had no views, but they were not expected to express them. The family was still a microcosm of the monarchy and of the Church, where the head possessed absolute authority. Even progressive socialists like Otto Bauer defined a woman's task as being "to organize the home in such a way that her husband would find it a place of peace, privacy and comfort".[15] Apart from a very small number who had a function in the Social Democratic Party, even well-educated women were largely confined to the home. It was to take some time before a more liberal education, which incorporated the theories of such men as Alfred Adler, enabled a majority of Viennese women to speak with a voice of their own.

A different set of problems presented themselves in the case of Ernst Langenfeld. Helen Fox suspected that the Vienna Group was prejudiced against him because he was Jewish and wrote:

> He is a curious individual, with a very unprepossessing manner and way of talking...The Austrian Friends have rather got their knife into him and don't want to admit him, or not now at all events, but I fear there is an anti-Semitic tendency among our dear friends there, suspicion and mistrust rather than active opposition. However, there may, of course, be things I don't know of, and, doubtless, care should be taken in dealing with the case.[16]

As far as can be gleaned from the records, Ernst Langenfeld never became a member of the Society of Friends. Whether this was because he lost interest or whether it was due to the attitude of other members of the group cannot now be ascertained.

One applicant had affinities with another large minority group, the Czechs, of whom there were 120,000-150,000 in Vienna. Joseph Schindler came to the Adult School classes to learn English from Hans Schindler. Although the two young men had the same surname, they were not related and came from very different backgrounds. Helen Fox reported to the Committee in London that Jo was "a hairdresser from very homely almost sordid surroundings":

> But his gentle manner and cultured face show an innate refinement...he is a most regular attender at all the Quaker activities and has a real concern for the spiritual life of the community. He is very diffident about his own powers, but he has a beautiful, humble spirit, and has taken part very helpfully in the Meetings for Worship.[17]

Helen Fox warmly recommended his admittance to the Society. Her judgement appears to have been sound, since Jo Schindler remained a faithful Friend throughout the troubles of the next decades.

Although a report by Headley Horsenaill to the London Yearly Meeting in 1924 expresses a feeling of "much satisfaction" at the steady growth of the Vienna Meeting, "which now includes some fifteen members and over thirty regular attenders", this was, in fact, the beginning of a steady decline in numbers. Both the Vienna Group and the British Friends had lost some of their initial optimism, as they were forced to recognize more clearly the various difficulties inherent in the whole enterprise of "spreading the Quaker message" in Austria. Many of the difficulties had been there from the beginning, but it was only gradually that their full weight was felt. They were aggravated by ignorance on both sides and by the relative wealth of the foreign Quakers, which was resented by the impoverished Austrians. British Friends, for their part, tended to romanticize the Viennese character, overlooking the deep wounds which festered under the superficial gaiety presented to the outsider. Language difficulties and the inevitable insecurity caused by living in a strange culture caused many of the younger relief workers to avoid close contact with the Austrians so that some prejudices on both sides could not be overcome. In any case, most of the relief workers had no interest in Quaker spirituality and no intention of staying in Vienna for any length of time.

By 1924, the situation for Austria in general was looking better and it was no longer so dependent on foreign aid, so that the number of relief workers fell still further. The country seemed more stable, at least on the surface, and the economy was beginning to improve, although the number of unemployed kept on rising, from 127,000 in 1924 to 202,000 in 1926.[18]

In some ways, the outlook for Austrian Friends became more hopeful, too, in spite of the drop in numbers. They moved back to the palatial building in the Singerstrasse in 1924 and became better integrated into the activities organized by the Centre. They also joined the British and American Friends in supporting the Land Settlement Scheme. By this time, the Settlements had developed their own financial and material structures, so Friends directed their efforts towards building community centres in the Settlements, where people could meet on equal terms and overcome the barriers between them. By encouraging social activities there, Friends hoped to reconcile the various social, political and religious groups with one another.

In the Centre itself, new activities, also aimed at reconciliation between people from different backgrounds, were introduced. It has already been described how, at the peak of the famine, several hundred Viennese children had been sent abroad, many of them to England. On their return, Friends had set up ten clubs in various parts of the city to keep contact with these children. At first, these clubs had to be in the neighborhood of the children's homes, but as the children got older, it was decided to amalgamate the clubs into one, called the "Joint Club", which, in future, was to meet in the Centre, under the leadership of Christina Clarence Brown, a trained youth club worker brought specially from England.

Most of the young people were "Catholic in upbringing but practically all indifferent as far as conviction and practice went".[19] Many came from poor families where the parents worked long hours. In others, the parents and older brothers and sisters were all out of work, so that often the club members could not find the tram fare to come to the meetings. Because of Vienna's chronic housing shortage, many of the children lived in overcrowded flats consisting of one room and a kitchen.

> But Vienna does not wear her troubles on the surface, and although the economic prospects for her young people were of the darkest, driving many to despair, and not a few to seek their fortunes in other countries, those who appeared for Club evenings were healthy of body and mind, eager to learn as well as to play - a characteristic that would be lacking in a British group under the same conditions – and possessing the national gift for gay spirits and friendliness.[20]

When it came to deciding what the purpose of this club should be, Friends were divided once more. Some of the Friends on the Committee responsible for running the club felt that "the ultimate drawing of the young people into Meeting for Worship or into the Society itself alone justified the running of the clubs at the Centre". Others, while holding the view that the aim should be to inculcate a religious attitude to life rather than insisting on any specifically Quaker element, wanted to exclude any "secular" activities from the program. Carl Heath pronounced that "religion is not an instruction but communicated life". The aim of the club was finally defined as being " to develop personality by giving direction to thought, study and forms of recreation, and by fostering the spirit of comradeship and service in group life".[21]

> English lessons, discussions and lectures on different subjects and questions of common interest, sport, excursions, all provided by the club committee, are some of the many ways in which the members of Joint Club, whose number is about 70 now, try to reach these aims.[22]

Christina Clarence Brown tried to encourage the club members to take responsibility for the running of the club and to practise democratic procedures, but any attempt to interest them in religious matters failed.

More success in this area was achieved in the other youth club which met in the Centre, the "Forum Club". This was intended for a slightly older group, mainly students. It met on Tuesday and Friday evenings. On Tuesdays there were lectures in German, French or English on a wide range of subjects, on Fridays there were discussions, and at the weekends, there were excursions and social gatherings. The main purpose of the club was to enable students from different backgrounds and with different political convictions to meet on neutral ground and form personal friendships across the ideological barriers. Some of the students became interested in Quakerism, and about twenty of them formed a study group to learn more about it. Every year, one or two of them went to Woodbrooke for a term. Later, one of these, Otti Guttwillinger, became Clerk of the Vienna Meeting. Another, Grete Schnellar, married Rudi Böck and also became a member of the Society of Friends.

Headley Horsenaill's wife, Elizabeth, took charge of the hostel which was opened in the Singerstrasse in 1927 to house visitors from other countries, especially those Friends passing through Vienna to the countries of Central and Eastern Europe which were still struggling with the after-effects of the war. Many of the visitors were asked to talk about their aims and experiences, so that lectures over a whole range of topics could be offered at the Centre.

The Vienna Group paid a token amount for the use of rooms at the Centre and continued with their own program of classes and lectures. By 1926, the number of members had dropped to twelve, and the group was still struggling to become an independent body. A new issue arose that

Rudolf Böck in the garden of his house, which became the home of the first Viennese Quakers.
(VIENNA MEETING)

year when, at Easter, Rudolph Böck attended the first German Yearly Meeting at Sonnenfeld. He was very impressed by the "wonderful spirit" of the meeting and immediately afterwards wrote to Carl Heath, saying that he and his family and two other Members of the Vienna group who were at the meeting had reached the conclusion that "from the spiritual point of view it is much better to join the German Yearly Meeting...without acknowledging the artificial barriers of political boundaries".[23] Carl Heath replied:

> In a general way, I have very deep sympathy with the idea of a common meeting for Germany and Austria – spiritually that seems to be the natural thing, as some of us think it is politically.[24]

However, some of the Members insisted that they preferred the existing arrangement, and the idea seems to have been dropped for the time being. The reservations on the part of the Vienna Group may have stemmed from their close affinities with British Quakerism, as well as from differences of temperament, taste and tradition between them and the mainly Northern German Quakers, whose spirituality was influenced by the Lutheran ethic and based closely on the Bible.

Rudolf Böck tried to share responsibility for the Meeting with the other Members and persuade someone else to become Clerk, as his health was rapidly failing. By the date of the fifth Austrian Yearly Meeting in March 1927, he was seriously ill, but he was still determined to carry out a project dear to his heart. Having spent the summer term of 1924 in Woodbrooke, he was anxious to bring the tutors and former students of Woodbrooke to Austria for the Woodbrooke Reunion, which took place annually in various countries and towns. He made all the plans for holding the 1927 reunion in Vienna but he died suddenly on 11th April, a few months before it was to take place. It was left to his widow and son to complete the arrangements and entertain the visitors.[25]

NOTES
[1] *The Friend* 6th April 1923.
[2] Greenwood 1978: 251.
[3] Headley Horsenaill n.d.: 84. FHL.
[4] *Woodbrooke Journal 1930*: 26. Woodbrooke Library.
[5] ibid.
[6] Horace Alexander: *Private Files.* Woodbrooke Library.
[7] ibid
[8] ibid.
[9] *Minutes of the Foreign Membership Committee* FHL.
[10] *Woodbrooke Journal 1930*: 26. Woodbrooke Library.
[11] *Foreign Membership Committee Papers.* FHL.
[12] H.Clark to Carl Heath 1st June 1920 *Foreign Membership Committee Papers.* FHL.
[13] *Foreign Membership Committee Papers.* FHL.
[14] ibid.
[15] Quoted in Gruber H. *Red Vienna: Experiment in Working-class Culture 1919-1934* New York 1991.
[16] ibid.
[17] ibid.
[18] Stadler 1971: 123.
[19] Brown 1934: 7.
[20] ibid.
[21] *FSC Pamphlet 1934*: 6. FHL.
[22] ibid.
[23] *Foreign Membership Committee Papers.* FHL.
[24] ibid.
[25] *Woodbrook Journal 1927*: 6ff. Woodbrooke Library.

CHAPTER 6

Political Unrest

TO UNDERSTAND Quaker involvement in the next major crisis in Vienna, it is necessary to be familiar with some of the political developments in Austria in the years between 1926 and 1934.

The political antagonism between town and country, between "red" Vienna and the Catholic and conservative country districts, was intensified by the growth of para-military groups, which gave former officers and soldiers for whom there was no longer any employment a new identity and a sphere of activity, in which they could wear uniforms, wave flags and march each Sunday to the music of a military band.[1] By the terms of the Treaty of Saint-Germain, Austria was allowed to have a standing army of 30,000 men, with a limited number of small arms.[2] However, the para-military groups, which were generally attached to one or other of the various political parties, became numerically much larger than the army.

In 1928, reports from the British Military Intelligence in Austria estimated that one of them, the *Heimwehr* (Home Defence) association, a para-military organisation which opposed parliament and the democratic constitution, was 107,000 strong and much better equipped and trained than the Socialist *Republikanischer Schutzbund* (Republican Defence League), which had about 100,000 members.[3] A year later the Heimwehr was said to have 350,000 members, and the *Schutzbund* 300,000. The former was, by this time, even more heavily armed. The army and the police were said to be in sympathy with the "extreme or fascist elements" in the *Heimwehr*, which was preparing to seize power by force if the Social Democrats should again become members of the Government. In spite of its anti-semitic leanings, the *Heimwehr* also had the support of leading bankers and industrialists,[4] many of them Jewish, who feared the effects on their business of a Socialist advance. In 1930, the *Heimwehr* put forward its own candidates at the election and won eight seats in Parliament. It then put pressure on the conservative government to increase its hostility towards the Social Democrats, who became afraid for the survival of democracy and saw Vienna as a fortress threatened by hostile forces. The workers in all the industrial towns were becoming desperate because unemployment was rising, especially in the capital. A series of bank failures added to the miseries of small investors, and the world economic crisis hit Austria with full force from 1930 onwards.

After the break-up of the Habsburg empire, all the political parties in Austria, except the Communists, had been in favour of some kind of union with Germany, because they were doubtful whether Austria could survive on its own, but enthusiasm for the idea waxed or waned in accordance with the changing political and economic climate in Austria and in Germany.[5] On the German side, the idea of union with Austria was welcomed but not pursued very actively. However, the emergence of National Socialism as a serious political force in Austria in the regional elections of 1932 changed the pattern of political life, and, with Hitler's coming to power at the end of January 1933, a new phase began in Germany, too, one which was much more aggressive and direct than the earlier *Anschluss* policy. As a result, the Austrian Social Democrats no longer supported the idea of union with Germany and removed it from their political programme.

A new chancellor, Engelbert Dollfuss, a member of the conservative party, had taken office in Austria on 20 May 1932. He made several fruitless efforts to conciliate the National Socialists and to negotiate with them. But no such efforts were made toward the other larger opposition party, the Social Democrats, although its leaders indicated their willingness to help in the fight against National Socialism. To Dollfuss, the "Reds", who were gaining in popularity, were the real enemy, and not the National Socialists. He therefore aimed at abolishing parliamentary democracy and at introducing an authoritarian "corporate" system, the *Ständesstaat*.[vi]

By means of a procedural trick, he suspended Parliament on 4th March 1933. With the backing of the Italian fascist dictator, Mussolini, and the *Heimwehr*, he set about removing the most serious obstacle to his plans, the Social Democratic Party, which, at that point, was the largest single party, representing 42% of the electorate. A series of repressive measures were passed, curtailing the freedom of the press and weakening the democratic constitution. The compulsory attendance at Catholic religious instruction for those children who did not belong to an established church was reintroduced, as was the death penalty, both of which had been abolished in 1919. Those who did not belong to one of the recognised churches were excluded from higher education, so that many people registered with one or other of these churches in order to avoid such discrimination.[7] For almost a year, the Socialist leaders tried by constitutional means to oppose this government, which, unlike that of Hitler in Germany, did not even attempt to acquire the semblance of legal or constitutional backing. The Socialists clung desperately to the hope that democratic methods, which had, in fact, already lost their relevance, would prevail.

One of the leaders of the *Heimwehr*, Major Fey, who was now also Minister for the Interior, tried to provoke the Socialists into beginning an armed revolt. At the end of March, a government decree declared that the *Schutzbund* was to be dissolved throughout Austria. The expected reaction from the Socialists did not take place. The Socialists decided that they would offer no armed resistance unless the Vienna Municipal Council were to be dissolved, or the trade unions and the Social Democratic Party forbidden. Next, the taxation system was altered by government decree, so that the Municipal Council of Vienna was deprived of much of its income. The housing programme could no longer be carried out, and wages in the public sector had to be curtailed.[8]

A letter to *The Friend*, written on 10th February 1934, sounded a prophetic note:

> The failure of the democratic countries to give efficient help to Austria has increased the influence of Italy on Austrian internal affairs. Italy desires that Austria should go Fascist, not Nazi. The plan of Dr Dollfuss is, in reality, an attempt to introduce Italian fascism into Austria, with a Roman Catholic tinge to it. Here is the weakness of the Dollfuss plan. It is an attempt to cast out the devil by Beelzebub! To all neutral observers in Austria, it is obvious that the right way to fight the Nazi danger would be by democracy, namely the rallying of all forces believing in Liberalism and Parliamentarism.[9]

The warning was not heard. On 11th February 1934, the day after this letter was written, Major Fey held a threatening speech, again aimed at provoking the Social Democrats. The police planned raids on Socialist buildings where arms were thought to be hidden. In response, the leader of the local section of the *Schutzbund* in Linz threatened to put up armed resistance should the police attempt to carry out such a search there. That evening Alois Jalkotzy, the secretary of the *Kinderfreunde*, telephoned to the Hotel Schiff in Linz, one of the places where the *Schutzbund* had hidden some weapons, to pass on a coded message, attempting to prevent any futile violence. He said, "The health of Uncle Otto and the aunt will be decided tomorrow. The doctors recommend waiting and not doing anything for the moment". This telephone message was intercepted and passed on to the police, whereupon it was decided to begin the search for weapons in Linz, not in the Park Baths, as had been intended, but in the Hotel Schiff instead. Members of the *Schutzbund* resisted the search, and fighting broke out.[10]

The disturbances spread to the main Socialist strongholds, including Vienna, and the Party leaders called for a general strike. However, the government forces, army, police and *Heimwehr*, far outnumbered the workers, and within three days the uprising had been crushed. Many of the "people's palaces" were severely damaged in the fighting; thousands of Social Democrats were arrested, even many who had not been involved in the fighting; nine of the *Schutzbund* leaders were hanged, whereas the political leaders escaped to Czechoslovakia at the beginning of the fighting. Hilda Clark sent Dollfuss a message, appealing for clemency:

> Quaker International Service, London, having a special interest in Austria through child-feeding 1919-1922, hearing with deep sorrow of suffering in your country, urges policies of mercy, especially with regard to repeal of death sentences.[11]

Edith Pye, as Chairman of the International Executive of the Women's League for Peace and Freedom, sent a similar message.

The Social Democratic Party was outlawed, socialist organisations disbanded, and their property confiscated, including buildings belonging to the *Kinderfreunde*. In Vienna over 102 children's homes, kindergärten and recuperation centres were handed over to a Catholic organisation called *"Frohe Kindheit"* (Happy Childhood).

Most of the families of those who were imprisoned or exiled were living in desperate poverty. Many Socialists, including 1200 who had worked for the gas and electricity companies, which had been the first to strike, lost their jobs and many were told that they were no longer eligible for unemployment benefits.[12] On 20th February 1934, Emma Cadbury wrote to her brother, describing the terrible situation:

> The papers gave the number of dead as 102 on the government side and 137 "civilians", with 319 wounded on the government side and 339 on the "civilian" side. Someone today reported 1600(?) dead, and 3000 arrested. Many are unemployed among the Social Democrats, and the wives of those arrested cannot draw their husbands unemployment dole, nor is any wage paid to those who had work, while they are in prison. As the party has been dissolved with the various organizations pertaining to it, many have thereby suddenly lost their jobs. In addition to this the Socialists in municipal employ are many of them losing their jobs at short notice. Whether they will receive the dole or pension is uncertain. Most of the workers had no savings. The apartment houses were not as badly destroyed as at first reported but many people lost their furniture and some flats were rendered uninhabitable.[13]

It is generally accepted that the official figures for those killed were far from the truth. The Socialists themselves estimated their dead at between 1500 and 2000, including a high percentage of women and children, and those wounded at 5000.[14]

A charitable fund was set up for the wives and children of those involved in the fighting, under the patronage of Frau Dollfuss, the wife of the Chancellor, and Cardinal Innitzer of Vienna, but people did not trust them. When they received food parcels from this fund, they were often presented with a form to sign, making them members of Dollfuss's new political organisation, the *Vaterländische Front*, which replaced the trade unions in Austria. They were afraid that they might be compelled to give information as to the whereabouts of those Social Democrats who were still in hiding. Emma Cadbury reports that they also feared "that their children will be taken from them and put into Catholic homes or monasteries and convents".[15]

The Labour Party in England joined in the appeals to Dollfuss to show clemency, but in vain. The Trade Unions abroad wanted to come to the assistance of the Austrian workers and collected money for them, especially in Switzerland, England and France. The Secretary of the International Trade Union Council, Walter Schevenels, and other leading officials travelled to Vienna and consulted Friedrich Scheu, the Viennese correspondent of the London newspaper, *Daily Herald*, about how best to organise the distribution of the funds. Friederich Scheu, whose parents had been associated with the Quakers since the early days of the relief work, immediately recommended the Quakers at the Vienna International Centre, pointing out that they had demonstrated their efficiency and impartiality during the famine. He offered to ask Emma Cadbury whether the Quakers would agree to help.

Emma Cadbury wrote to her brother:

> Well, you can imagine that it is difficult to refuse to help in this great need if we really are the only channel of relief for many of those most bitter and fearful...If we decide to do this and get permission we shall probably telegraph to the AFSC. We have London's approval if it seems necessary, and Dr. Hilda Clark wires that she expects to be here Thursday night to advise with us and bring news from London.[16]

After consultation with Friends in London and Philadelphia, Emma Cadbury and Headley Horsenaill agreed to take on the task, and temporary helpers set out from London. Emma Cadbury welcomed the idea that Hilda Clark, now Chairman of the Austria and South-East Europe Committee of the Friends' Service Council in London, would come to assist her with the organisation of the work.[17] A few days later Hilda Clark arrived in Vienna, and the negotiations with the various officials began.

Even Dollfuss agreed to the scheme, although he tried to insist that it should be carried out in co-operation with a government or Catholic relief organisation. Naturally, those who received help were anxious that the police should not get hold of their names, and the socialist groups abroad threatened to stop sending money if the government tried to get hold of the lists of names. At first, the authorities did attempt to force the Friends to let them see the names, but this they steadfastly refused to do. In March, three Quaker women were arrested but released after a few hours.[18] Eventually, the harassment died down, and the Friends were able to continue with the relief.

In the first few months, about 8000 families received support. As well as regular sums of money, the Friends also gave out milk, fuel, clothing and shoes.[19] By the beginning of November 1934, they had distributed 1,215,872 Austrian Shillings. The number of families needing support gradually fell after that, so that by December 1936 it was only 222.

Some of the young people from the Joint Club and the Forum Club helped with the distribution, but the main work was carried out by about a hundred young socialists, men and women, many of them former leaders of the *Kinderfreunde* groups, who were now out of work. It was a stroke of genius to make use of these young people, as they were known and trusted by the families to whom they took the relief money.

Just as they had done at the time of the famine after the war, various organisations in several countries, especially Switzerland, offered to take groups of poor children and restore them to good health. It was planned to pay the cost of transport for 3000 of them from the Friends' funds. In fact, only 791 children were able to take advantage of the plan, since the government forbade further transport, as it was feared that the children would be subjected to "Marxist propaganda". The Quaker Centre then organised summer camps within Austria for the other children. Two convalescent homes belonging to the Lutheran Church were used, and several of the unemployed mothers were given work there, looking after the children.[20]

The Spectator reported on 9th March that "with their bullet-scarred tenements to remind them of the recent past, many of the workers are disposed to join the Nazis out of sheer anger against the Heimwehr, and whoever controls the Austrian Nazis (whether from Austrian soil or German) is showing some astuteness in giving an all-quiet order for the present". Many of the Socialists who had fled to Germany joined the National Socialists there. Others went just over the border to Brünn in Czechoslovakia, where they reorganised and went on publishing the socialist newspaper, the *Arbeiterzeitung*, which was forbidden in Austria. From there, it could easily be smuggled into Austria.

In an interview with his son, one of the men who took the fortnightly sums of money from the Quaker funds to the poor families describes how such visits were used to keep the numerous "illegal" socialist groups in touch with one another and reorganise them into a centralised body, the "Revolutionary Socialists", who swore to go on with the struggle against fascism:

> Comrade Fritz Jahnel was also one of the people working in the Singerstrasse. He had some function in the organization of the illegal Revolutionary Socialists. I put myself at his disposal, and my work consisted of taking copies of the illegal *Arbeiterzeitung* to the foreign correspondents. One of them was Friederich Scheu[21]...I think he worked for the Daily Herald...[22]

Among the families which received relief and the illegal newspaper in this way was that of Franz Jonas, who later became President of Austria.[23] After being kept in prison for fourteen months, he lost first his job and then the right to unemployment benefits, so that his family was totally dependent on the small amounts they received from the Quaker funds.

Friederich Scheu claims that the Quakers were aware that the Socialists were reorganising and keeping in touch with their members through the distribution of the funds, but, "like the famous one-eyed English Admiral Lord Nelson, they turned a blind eye to what they did not want to see. Their little religious sect had been persecuted for centuries and therefore had a traditional sympathy for the oppressed".[24]

Apart from Vienna, other towns in the provinces, especially in Styria, were also suffering great need. Once again it was necessary to concentrate on feeding the children. Emma Cadbury reported to her friends in America that food kitchens had been set up there, food parcels were being distributed, and about forty girls were employed to sew clothes from material donated by the local shops. The authorities and private people "are co-operating very helpfully and remember our service after the war".[25]

On 6th October 1934, an article in the *Arbeiterzeitung* reported that, apart from the money handed out to the needy socialist families, funds were also being used to send 56 women and 41 children to Russia. In the Friends' report for 1936, which lists the sums spent in the period between February 1934 and December 1936, there is an item which reads "144 families (196 people) were sent to their husbands or fathers in Russia". For propaganda purposes, the families of these exiled Social Democrats were at first greeted in Russia with great pomp and enthusiasm, and a special school with Austrian teachers was provided for the children in Moscow. However, tragedy later caught up with them again. Many disappeared into Russian labour camps, some were imprisoned and killed on Stalin's orders, while others, including children, were killed by the

Nazis or used by them as spies. Only a few managed to return to Austria during the Second World War.[26]

Many of the party leaders and officials, as well as the heads of the various socialist organisations, had been arrested. At first, it was planned to try them for treason, but eventually many of them were released, after having signed a declaration that they would not engage in any further political activity.

A report on the Friends' activities for 1935 notes:

> In May there was an extensive and very welcome amnesty whereby men who were serving sentences up to as much as five years were released, under probation for a period of five years. This has meant a reduction of 209 in the number of families who were dependent on us because their breadwinners were in prison, and indicates also that they promptly received unemployment insurance again... We are planning to send about 130 children this summer again to a holiday home in Austria.[27]

Many of the Schutzbund activists remained in prison or in a detention camp in Wöllersdorf, about twenty miles south of Vienna. Some were brought to trial in April 1935, when their defence was that they had fought to defend the constitution and that it was the other side which should have been accused of treason.[28]

In the midst of all these tribulations, the Quakers tried to maintain a spirit of goodwill and an impartial attitude towards all of the population, regardless of the political affiliations of the individuals with whom they came into contact. From the beginning of its existence, the Vienna Centre had drawn together people from all the social and political groups and offered a neutral meeting place where discussions could take place without resort to violence. While showing understanding for the problems facing the country, Friends went on stressing their belief in the fundamental unity of humankind and the basic dignity and worth of every human being. These views were suddenly put to the test once more.

NOTES
[1] Carsten 1977: 298.
[2] Zollner 1961:496.
[3] Carsten 1986: 129.
[4] ibid.: 137f.
[5] Schausberger 1988:113ff.
[6] ibid.: 130.
[7] Bock 1999: 74.

[8] Speiser 1979: 68.
[9] *The Friend* 16th February 1934.
[10] Stadler 1974: 18.
[11] *The Friend* 23rd February 1934.
[12] Gulick 1976: 504.
[13] Emma Cadbury to Henry Cadbury, 20. February 1934, AFSC.
[14] Gulick 1976: 496.
[15] Emma Cadbury to Henry Cadbury, 20. February 1934, AFSC.
[16] ibid
[17] London Yearly Meeting Report 1934.
[18] Hall 1938: 169
[19] Gulick 1976: 503f.
[20] Lehner M.S.n.d.: 52.
[21] Friedrich Scheu and his wife fled from Vienna in 1938 and lived for a short time with the Clark family in Street.
[22] Lehner M.S.n.d.: 51.
[23] ibid.: 57.
[24] Scheu 1972: 178.
[25] Report by Emma Cadbury, 29 March 1934, AFSC.
[26] Stadler 1974: 275ff.
[27] Report of the Vienna Centre 1935.
[28] Gulick 1976: 506f.

CHAPTER 7

Despots, Dictators and Despair

ON 25TH JULY, 1934, the Austrian National Socialists attempted an unsuccessful putsch to overthrow the government, during which they forced their way into Chancellor Dollfuss's office and shot him. The conspirators refused to allow anyone to enter the building, so that he died two and a half hours later, without the ministrations of a priest or a doctor. Although the revolt had spread to other parts of Austria, it was soon crushed and the leaders were imprisoned and later executed.[1]

Whereas Mussolini concentrated his troops on the frontier to show Germany that he would oppose any intervention, Hitler imposed restraint on the Austrian Legion in Germany and distanced himself from the Nazi acts of terrorism in Austria; he had decided that the time was not yet ripe for armed intervention.

Under Dollfuss's successor, Chancellor Schuschnigg, there was no return to democracy, and the repressive policies of the *Ständestaat* were continued. This time it was the Nazis who were forced to flee. About a thousand people known to be National Socialists were imprisoned in Vienna or held in the detention camp in Wöllersdorf., and several thousands were arrested in Carinthia and Styria. Soon, their families, too, were in need of help. Rudi Böck, who had been visiting Socialist families in Styria to distribute relief, reported to Emma Cadbury that the families of the imprisoned Nazis were equally hungry.[2] By September, 14,000 people, Socialists, Communists and Nazis, were being held in detention camps. People were frightened to put their names on any lists, in case they fell into the hands of the authorities.

In August, Emma Cadbury received a visit from a Protestant pastor, who had just come back from Berlin, where he had been to talk to members of the government there on the possibility of giving help. He had received Emma's address from Corder Catchpool, the FSC representative in Berlin. The pastor told her that "in Leoben 3000 Nazis were in prison, and in Klagenfurt 3000-4000, and that the women and children were very badly off and needed money and food".[3]

Emma Cadbury decided to take the concern to the German Yearly Meeting, which was being held that same month in Bad Pyrmont. Most of people attending it were not convinced that Friends ought to attempt the task of caring for the families of Nazis. Some Friends suggested that the Protestant Church would be the best agency for distributing relief, as they had a network of parishes in those districts which were most affected. However, according to Headley Horsenaill,

> the Protestants were fearful that if they undertook the administration of relief, some of which would go to Catholics as well as Protestants, for it is by no means only Protestants who have been Nazi - or at any rate pro-German sympathizers – that they would be suspected of trying to proselytize from the Catholics. You may know that since the February revolt, some 16,000 have joined the Protestant Church. The established Protestant churches – or some of their clergy at any rate – seem inclined to regard the present Catholic regime as aiming to ultimately stamp them out – in a sort of counter reformation. It seems, however, that this is an exaggerated view, and that it is only because of their political connections that they are in trouble. The majority of them have, undoubtedly, been Nazi-sympathizers, even though they have not been involved in this last "Putsch". As a matter of fact, one of the men hung for the murder of Dollfuss was a Protestant and received the last ministrations from a Protestant pastor.[4]

Some influential Quakers, including Carl Heath, Rufus Jones and Hans Albrecht, the Clerk of the German Yearly Meeting, happened to be attending a conference in Prague at the end of August, so Headley Horsenaill took advantage of the opportunity to bring the matter up once more. He found that there had already been some discussion about it in Berlin, where it had been decided that, if the Quakers were to be approached with the suggestion that they should administer funds, they could only agree to do so on condition that, like the February funds, the money should be given to all needy cases, irrespective of their political views.

There were, of course, additional difficulties this time. Although the Austrian government had originally put up with far more from the Nazis than it had from the Socialists, it seemed less likely that it would give permission for relief this time. Many of the Friends had reservations about accepting funds from any source connected with the German government, and it was also difficult to imagine who could be used to distribute the funds, even if they came from an acceptable source. Above all, there was the question of whether it would be right to distribute relief to persons with whose political ideas the Friends did not agree.

During the conference, another Friend, Gilbert McMaster, arrived from Berlin, bringing the news that a Mennonite representative of an organisation called "Brüder in Not", Professor Unruh, had come to the

Quaker Centre in Berlin, offering to put 50.000 German marks at Friends' disposal, which he said had been raised by his organisation for the relief of needy persons in Austria. He promised that more money could be raised throughout the winter and suggested that an appeal should be made to Friends in Germany and other countries for additional money and goods. He would make a similar appeal to American and Canadian Mennonites.

Carl Heath said that there were four points to be considered:

1. The source of the money, that is, whether it was certain that it did not come from German Nazi sources;
2. that it would be given unconditionally;
3. that the government of the country concerned (i.e. Austria) should agree to its administration;
4. that the Friends should reach clarity on the effects in Germany of the Quakers going to the assistance of Nazi sufferers in Austria, as obviously many Germans might misinterpret their help as approval of the Nazi regime. He stressed that this latter point should not be the determining factor, but it had to be considered. Hans Albrecht and the German Friends should think over what would be the results for them if this work were undertaken.[5]

Hans Albrecht was doubtful about the whole matter, especially when he heard that a large sum of money would be available each month from German sources. He pointed out that Germany was very poor and needed every penny for its own suffering people. Moreover, he was afraid that the Nazis might be using Friends for their own purposes.

Despite these objections, both Rufus Jones and his sister-in-law, Emma Cadbury, felt that it was an opportunity to demonstrate the impartiality to which Quakers had always laid claim. On 25th September, Emma Cadbury wrote to the Austrian President, asking for his approval of a plan to assist the families of the imprisoned Nazis:

> We suppose that you have been acquainted with the ground of our work; and indeed, that we want, out of Christian love, to help all our fellow men who find themselves in dire need, without making distinctions of race, nationality or political affiliation, and, second, that we feel this help to be particularly necessary where the suffering and despair of women and children may lead to bitterness, hate and eventually forceful excesses, which mean a danger not only for the safety and welfare of the country involved but also for the peace of other lands.

However, it seems to have been impossible to get a clear answer from any member of the Austrian Government. The matter dragged on until February 1935, when Gilbert McMaster wrote to Clarence Picket in Philadelphia:

> I do wish that Vienna could see its way clear to help the families of those who had to flee Austria in July last year... It is not going to be easy to go on working for the one side, and not helping the families of the other side, who are also suffering. I shall have to tell the "Brüder in Not" now very soon that we cannot accept their contribution. This will not be easy for me to do, and will not better our position here[6].

In the meantime, from December 1934 onwards, the time and energies of the foreign workers and the rest of the staff at the Vienna Centre was becoming more and more occupied with the problems of the refugees who were fleeing in ever increasing numbers from Germany, as the persecution of people opposed to the Nazi regime intensified. A voluntary welfare worker, a Jewish woman called Frau Kafka, came to the Centre three mornings a week to interview the cases and suggest what could be done to help them, but nevertheless much of the work had to be done by Headley Horsenaill and the office staff, especially Käthe Neumayer, the invaluable Austrian secretary, who had been employed there since 1921.[7]

Horsenaill also offered the use premises to a Committee made up of representatives from 20 organisations, which met regularly to discuss the problems of these refugees. He was both Chairman and Secretary of this Committee, which endeavoured to raise funds for the refugees and to better their status with the authorities. It was no easy task! The membership of the Committee was heterogeneous, and the attitude of the Government towards its endeavours was "rather uncordial".[8] As the relief work increased, the old man who had been doing the bookkeeping of the Centre since 1922 and who was by this time only working on a part-time basis, was unable to cope, and Headley Horsenaill had to take on this task, too. Friends were still administering funds for the Socialist families, some of whom were in great need. Many men who had not been able to serve their sentences earlier because the prisons were too full now had to go to prison, leaving their families without support.[9] It was, therefore, not surprising that the interest of the workers at the Centre in pursuing the complicated task of offering help to Nazi families, too, was not very great, and the matter was finally dropped.

The hostel at the Centre, to which people from all over the world came, enabled Emma Cadbury and Headley Horsenaill to keep in touch with what was going on outside Austria and to retain a sense of balance in an atmosphere which was becoming more and more claustrophobic. For the sake of the many foreign visitors, the Sunday Meetings at the Centre was normally held in English.

Meanwhile, the small group of Austrian Friends had gone on struggling with its own difficulties. As we have seen, it had proved impossible from the beginning to attract more than a handful of people who were prepared to make Quakerism the centre of their lives, although there were plenty who were vaguely interested in Quaker ideas and who could be counted on to turn up for lectures or social evenings at the Centre. The Vienna Friends went on with the Study Groups and sometimes held their own lectures, but the themes seemed to have been chosen haphazardly and even the members themselves attended only sporadically.

A British Friend, Bernard Lawson, whose contact with the members of the group went back to its beginnings during the famine, was disappointed when he visited them in April 1931 to find that they had not become more independent. He saw, however, how the struggle to survive in harsh conditions sapped their energy and he discussed possible solutions with them. One of the most loyal members of the group, Jo Schindler, the hairdresser, told him:

> I work 70 hours per week in my shop and when Sunday comes, I have little inclination to go to the town for a Meeting - I must get out somewhere.[10]

Having lived in Vienna long enough to become acquainted with the people's customs, Bernard Lawson knew that it was a long-standing tradition for the Viennese to go on all-day outings on Sundays, "something which to the Austrian is more than a mere excursion and which seems to minister to his deeper self".[11] He encouraged the group to be adventurous and try out new ideas. As a result of these deliberations, the Vienna Friends started holding Meetings for Worship in the Vienna Woods whenever the weather permitted.

Bernard Lawson also encouraged the Friends to consider how closely they should follow American and English traditional Quaker practices. He thought that if they could move away from the Centre once more and find a different time and place for their Meetings, they would be able to try out new methods which might be more suited to life in Austria He suggested that this might mean starting Meetings with some music or proceeding them with a short discussion or reading. He came to the conclusion that "the group would gain by allying itself with the German Yearly Meeting rather than regarding its spiritual fathers as being either across the Channel or the Atlantic Ocean". He also noted that

> we are up against the Austrian temperament - exceedingly friendly and loveable but not one which easily accepts responsibility or shows initiative. Then there is also the Catholic background...but I was told that even among Protestant bodies in Vienna the driving force or "lead" usually comes from German sources.[12]

These deliberations led him to the conclusion that what the group needed above all was a strong leader, preferably a German and at any rate a man, otherwise he saw little hope of Quakerism surviving in Austria. He obviously had the Clerk of the German Yearly Meeting, Hans Albrecht, in mind. The call for a strong authority seems to have been in the air, as is often the case when old values have been destroyed and people's confidence in their own abilities has been weakened.

Three years later, with the creation of the *Ständestaat*, there seemed even less hope of attracting new members to the group because of the prevailing political circumstances. Although the *Ständestaat* had many of the external features of a fascist regime, such as a leader with extensive unconstitutional powers, a single party system and a repressive press policy, it was also trying to build up a distinctive identity with a Catholic orientation as a new "spiritual alternative" to Nazi Germany.[13] In theory, the new constitution still upheld the religious liberty guaranteed by the Treaty of St Germain, but in practice, there were severe disadvantages for all those who were not Catholic. To stop the flow of people leaving the Catholic church, it was made extremely difficult for anyone to give up membership of any of the established churches.[14] It is, therefore, not surprising that the group of Friends remained small.

Faced with apparently insoluble problems and living in a country where hatred, intolerance and violence seemed to triumph, the workers at the Centre, as well as the Vienna Group, were in danger of falling into a state of despondency and inertia. The strain of struggling on in such inauspicious circumstances was beginning to take its toll.

NOTES
[1] Jelavitsch 1987: 206f.
[2] Headley Horsenaill to Clarence Pickett 26th August 1934. AFSC.
[3] ibid.
[4] ibid.
[5] Report by F. W. Tritton: 3rd September 1934. AFSC.
[6] FSC/GE/5. FHL.
[7] Questionnaire submitted to the FSC Committee for Expenditure February 1936. FHL.
[8] FSC Report for 1936. FHL.
[9] *The Friend* 12 Oktober 1934.
[10] Report to FSC by Bernard Lawson, April 1931. (copy in the writer's possession).
[11] ibid.
[12] ibid.
[13] Reichhold 1984: 373.
[14] Rettenbacher 1992: 18ff.

CHAPTER 8

A Work Camp in Marienthal

WRITING TO HER friends in Woodbrooke, Ottilie Guttwillinger, a young Austrian English teacher who had spent a term there in 1931, tried to overcome her despair at the events of February 1934:

> We are by no means saved, for great misery has come over Austria again... We were full of hope, we were successful in many things. Almost everything was being done for the children, welfare work, housing schemes, just to mention one or two of the problems which were brought into realization. And now we have got so far, the Social-Democratic party has been abolished and the minority, the Christian Socialists, are ruling the country. What will become of Austria we do not know. But we do know that the good cannot be suppressed. We have nothing to fear, we can look towards a better time[1].

The Vienna Group, which was still largely made up of people with Socialist leanings, like Ottilie Guttwillinger, was devastated at the destruction of all the innovations in public health and social services that the Socialists had introduced. They searched for some way of helping those who were now left destitute.

Headley Horsenaill, too, felt the pressure of working under a repressive regime:

> Since the authoritarian Government assumed power in Austria in the Spring of 1933, and more particularly since the civil disturbances of February and July 1934, it has been necessary to be somewhat more careful in the choice of (lecture) subjects. The Union (F.I.S.U.) has, however, always avoided Austrian party politics – and the aim of the lectures has always been reconciliation and mutual understanding.[2]

Because of the ever-widening ideological gaps between the members of the various groups which attended the Centre and also because of the general atmosphere of despondency, Horsenaill was eager to find some new task which would help to bridge the differences and give everyone new hope. Hilda Clark's original idea of holding the various groups in

Vienna together by involving them in the Land Settlement Scheme had given them a common aim, but now there was no longer any money for such schemes.

One Socialist who had been associated with Friends since the early twenties, Alois Jalkotzy, had been imprisoned together with other Socialist leaders after the futile uprising in 1934, despite having tried to prevent the outbreak of hostilities. After his release in the summer of 1935, he spent a term at Woodbrooke. Encouraged by one of the tutors, J. S. Hoyland, who had always taken a special interest in Quaker work in Europe, he started to work out a scheme for "manual missionary service" among the unemployed in Austria.[3]

Jack Hoyland thought that the time had come to put what he called his "Franciscan Battle Plan" into operation. Like St Francis, he believed that a combination of prayer and humble service could transform people's hearts and teach them to love and respect one another across the barriers of class and nationality. According to his plan, young people, and older ones, too, were to be encouraged to work in a spirit of humility for people less fortunate than themselves. With this aim in view, he had originally got together a team of young Cambridge students for a work camp in India, but the scheme had had to be abandoned because so many difficulties cropped up that Jack Hoyland feared that they might be more of a liability than an asset to those they wished to help. After talking to Alois Jalkotzy, he decided to try a similar scheme in Europe instead, and the two men began making plans for a work camp in Marienthal, a particularly poor village not far from Vienna, where long-term unemployment was driving many into the ranks of the National Socialists.

On his return home in the summer of 1935, with his life's work for the benefit of the Viennese children in ruins, Alois Jalkotzy began testing the feasibility of Jack Hoyland's ideas. His project received the eager support of Headley Horsenaill and Emma Cadbury, both whom felt that it was the sort of plan they had been searching for. With the help of his friend, Rudi Böck, Jalkotzy approached the Austrian government and got permission to make use of a scheme, called the Voluntary Labour Service (*Freiwilliger Arbeitsdienst*). This scheme had been introduced by the government in 1932 for the purpose of keeping unemployed persons occupied, particularly those whose unemployment benefit had expired. They were to work on public projects and receive a minimum recompense for their work. Most of the funds allocated to the scheme were spent on building roads and a few houses, but the government also allowed money to be spent on the establishment of subsistence settlements, especially on the outskirts of towns and cities, where the unemployed were to be given plots of ground on which to grow food. It was hoped that this would keep them from swelling the numbers of unemployed drifting into the cities.

Voluntary labourers working on such settlements were to be given up to two Austrian shillings a day for a maximum period of a year and a half.[4]

At first, the Social Democrats had opposed the idea of the Voluntary Labour Service, regarding it as the introduction of a form of slave labour, but now, in the changed circumstances, with unemployment reaching even higher levels, they felt it was legitimate to use every possible means of combating it.[1]

The village of Marienthal was already well known because it had been the subject of the first systematic sociological study of the effects of long-term unemployment. The three sociologists who had carried out this study, were, like many other prominent socialists, forced to flee the country after 1934. One of them, Maria Jahoda, looking back on the aims which had inspired them, echoed Ottilie Guttwillinger's words when, in an interview recorded in 1983, she said sadly:

> In Vienna we lived with the great illusion that we would be the generation of fulfillment, that our generation would establish democratic Socialism in Austria. Our whole lives were based on this fundamental idea. Today, there is no doubt that this was an illusion, but there is also no doubt that this illusion was constructive and enriching to life.[5]

The people who had been the object of these studies were in a worse state than ever after the events of 1934. The whole village had been built around a textile factory, with large spinning mills where nearly all of the adults were employed. There were about 1500 inhabitants, with about 300 children among them. The houses there were built by the factory owner and originally they were tied to employment in the factory. When the factory was forced to close in 1929, 1100 men became unemployed. They and their families could not move to the city in search of employment because they could not risk losing their housing, although they were untrained for work on the land. In 1932, a Czech bought and re-opened part of the factory, employing only 140 people, most of them women, at very low wages, about half of what they had received before. Anyone not employed at the factory now had to pay rent for the house. Since there was no chance of further employment in Marienthal itself, the poverty of the inhabitants was extreme, and they lived for years on the edge of starvation. Unemployment relief got progressively less, the longer someone was out of work. At the end of twenty-five weeks it was cut off entirely, and people went onto public assistance, which was extremely low. No dole was given to anyone under twenty-five years of age. This meant that it was impossible for most of the young people to marry and start a family, which accounted for the relatively few children in the village.[2] About twenty of the young men were eligible for employment by the Voluntary Labour Service. The Government not only agreed to the scheme but it also provided competent agricultural experts to advise on how to make the scheme work.[3]

Having got the co-operation of the government authorities, Rudi Böck and Alois Jalkotzy contacted Jack Hoyland to stir up the enthusiasm of the young students in England. They hoped to get about six people to go, but, in fact, sixty-six volunteered, even though they had to find the funding for the thirty days they spent abroad. If necessary, they were expected to "do their own begging".[6]

The first group of English students arrived in Vienna in the summer of 1935, travelling by steamer down the Danube. The aim, in accordance with Jack Hoyland's vision of the sacramental nature of physical work,[4] was for them to work side by side with the unemployed, to show them how to better their economic situation and, at the same time, to give an example of practical reconciliation by demonstrating that human fellowship is able to overcome all differences of class, nation, education and wealth.

First of all, the men students were to help the unemployed to reclaim land by dredging a river and draining a swamp and then to prepare allotment gardens for between forty and fifty families, as well as a common plot for the growing of potatoes. In addition to these efforts towards an improvement in the diets of the unemployed, they were also to prepare the ground for growing medicinal herbs. A contract with a firm supplying medicines had already been secured. The women were to do domestic work, not only in the camp but also in some of the homes.

The students were shocked at the conditions in which the people lived:

> The housing conditions are dreadful. Before we left England, we wrote asking that we might live in the homes of the unemployed men, as we always do in work camps in England and Wales. But the answer came that this was impossible "on moral grounds". We did not know what this meant until we actually came to live in Marienthal, when we found that six or eight persons often live in a single room, and even ten or twelve is not uncommon.[7]

It was then arranged for the students to live in the building that had formerly belonged to the *Kinderfreunde*. To show the students that the Social Democrats had had a different vision of housing, Rudi Böck took them to see the exemplary workers' flats which had been constructed in Vienna before the Socialists were suppressed.[8]

One of the students, Graham Marquis, who went to the first work camp in the summer of 1935, describes how the students tried to live on the same amount as the unemployment benefit paid to the workers:

This paid for a diet of macaroni, cooked in a little butter, bread with caraway seeds, a tiny ration of jam, and nothing more. The Austrian villagers did seem very skinny and undernourished...[9]

Although the students only had to feed themselves and were in good condition at the outset, whereas the Austrians often had to keep a whole family and had been living on the edge of starvation for years, it proved too difficult for the students to maintain their health on the pittance they were given. They decided to supplement the diet with one good meal a day, which they shared with the Austrian workers. Even so, they found that the men had very little stamina. The students could work a great deal more steadily than the Austrians, who had, in some cases, eaten little but bread for several months. The psychological effects of long-term unemployment were also evident. The young Austrians felt that no-one had any use for them, and nothing was worth doing.

The students were also shocked at the political situation:

> "Tense" is hardly the word to use. The feeling in Vienna was such that no-one would have been surprised to wake up and find a revolution in full swing. The government probably only has 20% of the people behind it. The Socialists and Nazis are vigorously suppressed, but one feels they are only waiting for the opportunity for action. Each, of course, is opposed to the other, and both are opposed to the Catholic party in power... Anyone's house may be thoroughly searched by the police as a result of even anonymous letters sent to the police station denouncing an individual as a Nazi or Socialist. One of our friends in Vienna had had her house searched five times, and each time nothing had been found against her. Because she was „under suspicion" at the time of a university examination, she was not allowed to take it.[5]

All kinds of difficulties had to be overcome before work could begin on the allotments. The reasons for this were again political. Marienthal was part of the municipality of Grammat-Neusiedl, which was largely a peasant community. The peasants were all supporters of the government, whereas the former textile workers were mostly Socialists, so that there was a great deal of mistrust between them. In order to win the goodwill of the peasants, it was decided to start by improving some common land, used by them for raising cattle:

> The work was fairly heavy. Roots were dug up and land cleared and drained. The river was dredged and its banks raised, and at last we were permitted to prepare land for the actual allotments...The Austrian authorities could not decide whether we were Nazis or Socialists. The unemployed could not understand why English people should do work for which they would gladly have received wages. However, when the volunteers had been

there for a month, a really fine spirit grew up. This was in spite of the fact that individuals, few of whom could speak German, only spent about a fortnight each at the camp. The whole business lasted nearly three months, in which time over sixty volunteers had worked there with about seventeen Austrians and a permanent Austrian organizer.[10]

Misunderstandings also arose because of differences in life styles. The woman in charge of the students was a lively young Cambridge graduate called Mary Campbell. One day she cycled into Vienna, wearing rather brief shorts. A small disapproving crowd gathered round her, and she heard someone say, "Not even in England do they allow girls to cycle in shorts". Far from being disconcerted, she returned to Marienthal, bubbling with joy because no-one had suspected that she was not Austrian[11]. She won the respect of the Austrians by working in the fields as hard as any man, as well as doing domestic work, organising sporting events and leading the evening sing-songs. It was largely thanks to her cheerful leadership and her knowledge of German that the initial mistrust felt by the unemployed towards the foreign strangers, whose motives they could not understand, was quickly dispelled.

In the following two summers, when the experiment was repeated, efforts were made to improve the food rations, for both the students and the other workers. The Vienna Friends were encouraged by Alois Jalkotzy to do without one meal a week throughout the year and to give what they saved to the people in Marienthal to help them through the hard winter when there were no cheerful English students to share their burdens. Friends from the German Yearly Meeting sent clothing parcels and toys for the children.

Each year between sixty and seventy young people travelled from England to take part in the scheme. Of course, it did little towards solving the problem of long-term unemployment, but it helped the undergraduates to understand what it meant for those who had to live for years under the subsistence level, with little prospect of ever obtaining regular employment. It also showed them why so many people in Austria looked for help to Germany, which seemed to them a land of plenty, where under Hitler, unemployment had practically disappeared.[6] The unemployed could not be expected to understand that Hitler's schemes were directed towards controlling the whole economy in preparation for war.

Jack Hoyland was more than satisfied with the work camps, and so was Rudi Böck. His final verdict was:

> This work camp idea is inspired nonsense, and it succeeds. You send workers to an unemployed place, and they create work for the workless.[12]

Undergraduates helping unemployed Austrians to prepare the ground for vegetables and medicinal herbs in Marienthal 1936.
(DENNIS CONOLLY)

Cambridge graduate being seen off at the station near Marienthal.
(DENNIS CONOLLY)

One of the organizers from Cambridge wrote:
> One of the men said to me before I left, You know, before you came, we thought of England as a little country a long way off, with lots of colonies and therefore very rich, with no poverty and no unemployment...Now we know that England has all the problems that we have and that it is your home, we could not fight against you.

Unfortunately, they were soon to have little choice but to fight.

Soon after Hitler's annexation of Austria, Rudi Böck's wife, Grete Böck-Schnellar wrote to Woodbrooke:
> You will be interested to hear that some weeks ago the work camp in Marienthal has been liquidated by the Marienthal Committee for the most pleasant of reasons - that there is no unemployment there any more. You would be astonished to see how quickly things are changed, unemployment is disappearing in rapid steps and the want of trained workers is to be felt. Jack Hoyland will be glad to hear about Marienthal; he knows how great the misery has been there. As far as I know a great factory of artificial india-rubber, which is a very good product, will be built there and a big garden city for the workers[13].

The rubber factory was needed as part of the preparation for war, and the garden city remained a dream, as war broke out before the plan could be realised.

After the war, Jack Hoyland heard from the people in Marienthal that food from the allotments had saved them once more from starvation, when the area where they lived was overrun by the Red Army and became part of the Russian Occupied Zone[14]. The allotments provided almost everything they had to eat.

Jack Hoyland would have said that the value of the work should not only be measured in material terms. It gave everyone concerned something positive to work for, at a time when such signs of hope were rare. Even though those who took part in the work camp soon found themselves separated by the nightmare of war, their attitudes had been permanently changed by their shared experiences.[15]

NOTES
[1] Woodbrooke Journal, no. 27: 1934.
[2] Horsenaill M.S.: 148. Woodbrooke Library.
[3] Reynolds 1958: 68.
[4] Enderly-Burcel 1980: 352-54.

[5] Official statistics gave the official number of unemployed in 1933 as 26% of the potential labor force, but most historians today point out that large groups were missing from the official figures, such as the long-term unemployed and young people who had never had the chance of entering the labor market, so that a closer estimate would be 38%. See Ernst Brückmüller *Sozialgeschichte Österreichs* Vienna 1985: 500.

[6] Interview with Franz Kreuzer fifty years after the study on Marienthal in *Des Menschen hohe Braut: Arbeit, Freihzeit, Arbeitslosigkeit*, Wien 1983.

[7] "Nothing is more noticable in this place than the fewness of the children. The population has given up the struggle to survive, in despair" Hoyland MS: 7.

[8] Hoyland MS: 15.

[9] Hoyland MS: 13.

[10] "The Franciscan method of action works miracles of reconciliation, if only the spirit behind the action is right. It must be the Spirit of the Sacrament of the Feet-washing, pure from all self-seeking". Hoyland MS: 13.

[11] ibid: 9.

[12] ibid: 6.

[13] Marquis n.d.: 56.

[14] Hoyland MS n.d.:26. Woodbrooke.

[15] extract from an article written by G. Marquis in 1935 for his old school magazine.

[16] Letter from Graham Marquis 14.5. 99.

[17] For a detailed account of the effects of unemployment on the political situation in Austria see Carsten 1977:265f.

[18] Hoyland MS n.d.:32. Woodbrooke.

[19] G. Böck-Schnellar to Woodbrooke Journal 1938.

[20] Reynolds n.d.: 68.

[21] Over sixty years later, three of the English people who took part still remembered this work camp as having been a profound experience in their lives (letters from Dennis Conolly, Nicholas Gillett and Graham Marquis in the author's possession).

CHAPTER 9

Austria Abandoned

AFTER THE DISASTROUS turn of events in 1934, there were many pessimists who predicted a steady deterioration in the stability of the country. Without a reconciliation with the Socialists, Schuschnigg's authoritarian regime had little chance of checking the growing discontent, a situation which was exploited to the full by Nazi propaganda. One Quaker, returning to London from a visit to Vienna, reported in an article in *The Friend* in October 1934 that "an informed observer" had suggested to him that there were only two solutions now open, "either Anschluss with Germany or a restoration of the Habsburgs, and both mean war".[1] *The Times*, on the other hand, explained to its readers that "with the crushing of the Socialists, Austria is now set on a Fascist course",[2] whereas the historian E. H. Carr reported to the Foreign Office in London that

> independent Austria is dead, and the heir to her estate must be either Italy or Germany...In Austria itself, the Italian solution is supported only by the machine guns of the mercenary *Heimwehr*, and cannot therefore have the stability of the German solution...If the German solution is recognised as eventually inevitable, the sooner it comes, the better.[3]

The Austrians were not reassured by the attitudes of leading politicians in England, France and USA, who, having enough economic problems in their own countries, now wanted to wash their hands of all responsibility for Austria and its troubles.[4] Nor were they convinced by Hitler's solemn statement on 21 May 1935 that "Germany neither intends nor wishes to interfere in the internal affairs of Austria, to annex Austria or to conclude an *Anschluss*".[5] As was shown in the previous chapter, the unemployment rate remained high. As the buying power of the Austrian shilling fell once more, people looked with envy over the border to Germany, where, in contrast to Austria, unemployment had almost disappeared as a result of Hitler's planned economy and his preparations for war. Hitler intended war from the beginning, but at first he misled not

99

only the Austrians but also the Germans themselves. For years he talked of peace while preparing for war.[6]

Unemployment in Vienna was so bad that many hungry people committed petty crimes purely in order to get into prison and be given a meal.[7] However, as the Friends had recognised from the beginning, what people lacked as much as economic security was a belief in themselves and in their ability to come to terms with their difficulties. No Austrian identity had been found which could replace the vanished Habsburg empire and channel the energies and resources of the people into building up a viable state, and the Catholic Church, by supporting the overthrow of democracy and encouraging Austria's dependence on Italy, contributed to the bitter divisions within the country.

As to the economic situation, even during the period of superficial recovery and economic improvement from 1923-27, Friends had warned that beneath the surface all was not well and maintained their belief that the only solution for Austria was "back to the land" and the promotion of land settlements.[8] At that time, however, the Socialists in the Viennese Town Council had been afraid that they would lose the support of the workers once they had their own homes, so instead of encouraging the Land Settlement Scheme, they had tended to favour building huge housing blocks. Now that the ambitious schemes of the Socialists had been destroyed and the new authorities had assumed control, practically no new buildings were being put up.

One person had not lost faith in the Land Settlement idea. Rudi Böck had studied Architecture at the University of Vienna to prepare himself to follow the calling he had felt since his first acquaintance with the Quakers, when as a young boy he had witnessed the success of the Land Settlement Scheme in Vienna. It had made a lasting impression on him and determined his choice of a career. By 1935 he was working as an architect for the Vienna City Council, where the Housing Department was the only one which retained a Socialist as its Head.

In the early thirties, several of the Viennese Group had spent a term in Woodbrooke, and they kept up their contacts with the tutors there, so that the influence of British Quakers remained strong. However, Rudi Böck does not seem to have been a skilled linguist and he obviously found it easier to form ties with the newly formed German Yearly Meeting (GYM), instead. In 1933, he wrote to Carl Heath, telling him that, since the founding of the German Yearly Meeting (GYM), he had been studying the German roots of Quakerism and that these studies had brought him closer to German Friends. As a result, he wanted to transfer his membership of the Society of Friends from the London to the German Yearly Meeting.

When Bernard Lawson paid yet another visit to Vienna as part of his honeymoon in 1937, he attended a weekend gathering at which the Viennese Friends again tried to come to some decision about their future. Following the advice of several foreign Friends, they wanted to find a way towards greater independence, as the German Yearly Meeting had done. The discussions were lengthy and inconclusive, some of the members being reluctant to give up their membership of London Yearly Meeting and others wanting to form an independent Austrian Yearly Meeting.[9]

As the Austrian representative to the GYM from 1933 onwards, Rudi Böck attended the meetings of the German *Arbeitsausschuss*, the Executive Committee of the German Friends, and came under the influence of Hans Albrecht, the Clerk of GYM. Together they searched for ways to make Quakerism more acceptable to Germans by showing that Quaker spirituality was similar to that of the early German mystics. Both of them were convinced that George Fox had been influenced by the works of the

Bernard Lawson with his wife, Mary. He never lost faith in the Vienna Group even in the darkest days

(CHRIS LAWSON)

German mystics Jakob Böhme and Meister Eckhard. Amid the growing tensions after Hitler's coming to power in 1933, they stressed the spiritual aspects of Quakerism. Hans Albrecht tried to ensure the continued presence of the Society by proclaiming that the Friends had nothing to do with politics, and "it was on Hans Albrecht's initiative that Friends at the Frankfurt Quarterly Meeting in 1933 were advised to be selective about the time and issue on which to make a personal stand".[10] In April 1933, the Executive Committee circulated a letter to the members, reminding them that the Society of Friends was neither a pacifist organisation nor a charitable or humanitarian association but a religious society.[11] Rudi Böck, faithful to what he had learned from his father's old friend, Carl Heath, also insisted that Quakerism should be regarded not as creed which divides but primarily as "a way of life which unites".[12]

Both Hans Albrecht and Rudi Böck maintained their allegiance to the Quaker peace testimony in the face of pressure from other members of the German Yearly Meeting, one of whom put forward the view that if Quakers would give up non-violence, Quakerism could easily be the religion of the new Germany.[13] Another saw pacifism as a betrayal of the Fatherland and said that "some of the German pacifists have gone to the edge of *Landesverrat* (treason)".[14] During a discussion about the attitude of German Quakers to the new government, the wise voice of Carl Heath broke in to remind them that "Goebbels in the Sportpalast said that National Socialism had to be accepted as a whole, not in part".[15]

Meanwhile, Nazi propaganda continued to pour into Austria, and the absorption of Austria into Germany was one of the schemes that Goebbels had set his mind on. From Munich, he continually urged the Austrians to consider the advantages that they would gain from the new Germany's economic successes. Most Austrians needed no convincing that their country was not economically viable, and, in what seemed to be a choice between fascist Italy and Hitler's Germany, the majority certainly favoured Germany.

After the disturbances in 1934, the poor in Vienna could no longer rely on the excellent system of social services which the Socialists had slowly built up after the war. A Quaker visiting the city in 1937 describes the long tragic queues that stood waiting every day for food from the various soup kitchens around the city. Those who spent the night in shelters for the homeless had to leave at seven o'clock each morning, so that they were on the streets all day:

> They brought their own basins, usually old cocoa tins, and when they had been served they sat on the curb, or on the steps of neighbouring houses to eat. They warmed their hands round the tins of their steaming food.[16]

Realising that the situation was deteriorating, various well-meaning Friends from abroad travelled to Vienna and offered their help and advice, but they often had little understanding of the personalities and attitudes of the Viennese. In spite of their good intentions, they were often handicapped by linguistic shortcomings and cultural bewilderment, as well as by their ignorance of the historical background.

One of the more perceptive of them was an AFSC-representative at the Berlin Centre, Anne Martin, who picked up the general feeling of desolation and despair when she visited Vienna in February 1937. She talked to the Viennese Friends and commented:

> The Catholic Church is making its last stand here, and the people who do not work up enough independence to leave it are so bitter that most of them never want to hear the word "God" or "Christ" again - which is something that Emma and the good English Friends here can understand in theory, but can't quite swallow in practice. It would be a hard place to work. The very small group of Quakers here - twenty, of whom only eight are really active, with of course always a fringe of more or less interested attenders - are very dependent upon the Centre both materially and otherwise, - and real understanding is probably well-nigh impossible.[17]

She also witnessed some demonstrations on the occasion of an official visit by the German Foreign Minister, von Neurath, and tried to convey some of her impressions to her friends in the USA, trying to convey to them how vulnerable to manipulation the Austrians had become as a result of the extreme poverty which prevailed:

> Of the mob of 8,500 Nazis that greeted him Monday evening with "Hail (*sic*) Hitler" etc, 4,500 were brought in from the provinces; and for the demonstration the following evening, to demonstrate that the people were wedded to their government and Austrian independence, 40,000 miserable wretches - we saw several columns of them trudging through the streets, shivering in their patched coats and carpet-bag shoes - were brought in from the provinces, transport provided, of course, beer, sandwiches, and five shillings ($1) apiece. One reporter managed to work himself in through the police that surrounded them as they walked to the station in the evening, and talked with various men; and he heard various funny things, of course. For instance, one man asked his neighbour, "What is it we're supposed to yell?" to which the other replied, "I don't know - it's probably best to keep quiet".

A similar atmosphere struck the journalist William L. Shirer when he returned to Vienna at Christmas of the same year and noted that Vienna seemed terribly poor, compared to what it had been when he had lived there before from 1929 to 1932:

> The workers are sullen, even those who have jobs, and one sees beggars on every street corner. A few people have money and splash it at the night clubs...The contrast is sickening, and the regime is resented by the masses, who are either reverting to their old Socialist Party, which is fairly strong underground, or going over to Nazism. The great mistake of this clerical dictatorship is not to have a social programme. Hitler and Mussolini have not made that mistake.[18]

Like the Social Democratic Party, the National Socialist Party (NSDAP) was still officially forbidden as a political party. However, the National Socialists benefited from the worsening social climate and increased their propaganda, aimed at intimidating the government and fanning the latent anti-Semitism into new flame. In June 1937, 75,572 Austrians were members of the illegal party. By December, the number had risen to 105,035,[19] as the likelihood of a German take-over increased.

Chancellor Schuschnigg, alarmed by the lack of support for Austrian independence on the part of Mussolini, met Hitler at Berchtesgaden on 12th February 1938 and was subjected to bullying and humiliation. Finally, he agreed to grant a complete amnesty for all the imprisoned Nazis and to make the Austrian Nazi, Seyss-Inquart, Minister for the Interior, giving him control of the police. Almost immediately, the Nazis began street demonstrations, culminating in huge demonstrations in Graz and Linz, in the presence of the new Minister for the Interior.

Nevertheless, Schuschnigg, in a last attempt at preserving Austria's independence, planned a plebiscite for 13th March 1938, estimating that about three-quarters of the population would vote for an independent "Christian and united Austria". After long discussions, the Socialists decided to support the plebiscite. But it was too late. Hitler's reaction to Schuschnigg's plan was to send an ultimatum, demanding a postponement of the plebiscite. When German troops crossed the border on 12th March, Schuschnigg decided to offer no resistance. The next day, the *Anschluss* (the annexation of Austria) was proclaimed, and on the day that the plebiscite ought to have been held, the German army reached Vienna. Thousands of opponents to the Nazi take-over were now in danger, and many tried to flee the country as a terrible persecution began.

NOTES
[1] *The Friend* 13th October 1934.
[2] *The Times*, 17 February 1934.

3 Carsten 1986: 193.
4 When asked to grant Austria preferential treatment, especially with regard to the import of Austrian timber, the President of the Board of Trade in London, Runciman, replied that he could offer help only with regard to "velour hats, which he mentioned to show how little could be done. Our imports from Austria were down to a very low level". Quoting this episode, F. L. Carsten remarks, "It sounded like a bad joke". Carsten 1986:196
5 Seton-Watson 1938: 438.
6 "Die Umstände haben mich gezwungen, jahrelang fast nur vom Frieden zu reden. Nur unter der fortgesetzten Betonung der deutschen Friedenswillen und der Friedensabsichten war es mir möglich, dem deutschen Volk ...die Rüstung zu geben, die immer wieder für den nächsten Schritt als Voraussetzung notwendig war". *Speech of Hitler's to the German Press, November 1938.*
7 Marquis 1990: 55
8 CIS minutes 1921-25 and Minutes of the Vienna Sub-Committee of the Friends' Relief Council for 1923-27. FHL.
9 Lawson 1978: 22.
10 Corder Catchpool: handwritten notes on an Executive Committee Meeting (Arbeitsausschusssitzung) of the German Yearly Meeting 31.3. 1934 –1.4..34.FHL. See also Bailey 1994:
11 "Die Gesellschaft der Freunde ist keine Friedengesellschaft, kein Wohltätigkeitsverein oder humanitärer Bund irgenwelcher Art, sondern eine religiöse Gesellschaft". Quoted in Otto 1972: 297
12 Confidential Report to FSC by Roger Clark 1938. FHL.
13 Corder Catchpool: handwritten notes on an Executive Committee Meeting (Arbeitsausschusssitzung) of the German Yearly Meeting 31.3. 1934 –1.4..34. FHL.
14 ibid.
15 ibid.
16 Waln N. 1938: 224.
17 Anne Martin to AFSC 27th February 1937. AFSC.
18 Shirer 1941: 77.
19 Riedl 1992: 178.

CHAPTER 10

Darkening Skies

IN THE QUAKER Centre on the evening of 12th March, Emma Cadbury was quite unable to sleep, and at one o'clock she decided to use the night to describe her impressions of the fateful events of the last few days in a letter to her family. For some days there had been a series of demonstrations in Vienna, first by Nazi supporters, wearing the swastika and greeting one another with "Heil Hitler", then by people shouting for Schuschnigg and Austria. The streets were full of excited crowds, anxious to hear the latest news, and slips of paper were scattered everywhere, urging people to vote with a "Ja" in favour of an independent Austria in the forthcoming plebiscite. A series of speeches by members of the government was planned, but, instead, Schuschnigg made a brief announcement of the Government's resignation. The following day, Emma Cadbury went through the city on her way to the opera and saw that the majority of people were wearing Swastika pins, and many were carrying flags from which the Austrian emblem had been cut and replaced by the Swastika. Even prams and dogs were decorated, and the shop windows were full of pictures of Hitler. A military parade of the German army took place in the evening along the Ring, the main road surrounding the city centre, and there was no sign of any resistance.[1]

Friends in England and USA were alarmed for Emma Cadbury's safety, as they realised that the Centre might fall under the displeasure of the Nazis because of the support it had been giving to those who had fled from Germany since Hitler's coming to power. She was under considerable strain, struggling to help all the desperate people who were anxious to escape from Austria while there was still time. Since Headley Horsenaill had been forced to return to England in September of the previous year because of ill-health, she was also fairly isolated.[2]

The links between the International Centre and the Vienna Group, which had never been very strong, had been weakened still further by Horsenaill's departure, as he had always supported the group and believed in its potential for growth, whereas Emma Cadbury favoured the idea of a "Wider Fellowship", a loose-knit fellowship of those who sympathised

*Staff members at the Vienna International Centre Summer 1938.
Front Row seated from left: Elizabeth Yarnell; Emma Cadbury; Ethel Haughton;
Standing: Robert Yarnell; Mary Campbell; Hubert Butler; Brigit Kelsey Hodgkin.
The two Austrian workers, Käthe Neumayer and Franz Lipovsky, are not shown.*
(VIENNA MEETING)

with Quaker principles but who were not expected to become members of the Society of Friends. After Horsenaill's departure, the relationship between the Centre and the Vienna Group had worsened immediately, ostensibly because there were quarrels between the small Vienna Group and some members of a pacifist organisation, the *Weltjugendliga*, which had been forbidden by the police and given shelter in the Centre. Its members were allowed to meet in the Centre under the innocuous name of *Freundschaftskreis* (Friendship Circle). In November 1937 Rudi Böck had written to the Friends' Service Council, protesting that these pacifists had made fun of a talk on Quakerism that the Vienna Group had arranged and had shown that they had no real interest in it. He wrote that there was "a sense of competition" between the Centre and the Group, so that there was "no longer any co-operation between the Centre and the Vienna Group, except that the bookkeeping of the Group is done by the Centre".

He wanted an Austrian representative on the Centre's committee, who ought to have equal rights with the foreign representatives, as was the case in Berlin, but this suggestion seems to have been ignored.[3]

Thus, in the dangerous situation in which she now found herself, Emma Cadbury could not count on much support from the Viennese Quakers. Nevertheless, she reassured her family by telling them that both Hans Albrecht and Corder Catchpool were planning to come from Berlin and that she was also supported by two visiting American Friends. At Emma's request, the Austrian Committee of the Friends Service Council in London decided to ask Hilda Clark and a young Friend, J. Roger Carter, to go to her assistance and try to assess the personal danger she might be in. Another British Friend, Ann Stewart, was prepared to stay and give whatever assistance she could, and Louisa M. Jacob, who had worked in the Centre two years earlier, also returned to help with the relief work. Mary Campbell, who knew Austria from her work in Marienthal, came, at the suggestion of Bernard Lawson, to give support specifically to the Vienna Group, but she, too, found herself caught up into the office work, so that she was not able to find time for anything else.[4] One of the Vienna Group, Wilhelmine Otto-Ottenfeld, took over the bookkeeping.

Most of the previous work of the Centre came to an end, as no unauthorised organisations were allowed to hold lectures or organise club evenings. The personnel of the Centre was totally occupied with providing help and consolation for the people who were persecuted under the new regime or who knew that they would soon be put under pressure. The brutal treatment and humiliations meted out to many Jews immediately after the *Anschluss*, not only by the new rulers but also by that segment of the Austrian population which welcomed the opportunity to vent their racist resentment with impunity, increased the urgency. However, it became more and more difficult to get visas for many of the people registered with the Centre, and some saw suicide as the only way out. Those who feared for their lives felt that they had been left to their fate, as the governments of Europe and the USA raised no substantial protest against the annexation of Austria. The Nazi leaders were still treated as equals by other statesmen and some said quite openly that it was no concern of theirs what happened within Germany's borders. It looked as if Austria had disappeared for ever. It even lost its name and became the *Ostmark* (Eastern District of Germany).

On 10th April, when a plebiscite was held in which the population was asked to vote in favour of the *Anschluss*, almost 99% of those eligible to vote gave it their support. The Austrian bishops of the Catholic Church, under Cardinal Innitzer, issued a declaration, advising their flock to vote in favour, whereas the leaders of the protestant churches expressed their "sincere joy" over the *Anschluss* and saw their "YES" as a sign of "their sincere gratitude to a merciful God for saving and freeing our native country".[5] Even one of the leaders of the Social Democrats, Karl Renner, announced that he intended to give his vote in favour.[6] There is no question that such an overwhelmingly favourable result could not have been obtained without threats, propaganda and pressure, as well as by the exclusion of 360,000 people from the voting lists. Nevertheless, it gave the new rulers the appearance of legality.[7]

Emma Cadbury wrote to her family:

> Meantime, most of the leading men in Germany have been in Vienna and have given public speeches, and now the leader himself is back again in Austria for his second visit. We are quite used to the brilliant red flags with the swastika which floats from the housetops and windows or in smaller forms are displayed everywhere, to the swastika pins worn by German citizens who have the right to vote, to shrines to the leader and to his picture everywhere, and to the slogan, "Ein Volk, ein Land (*sic*), ein Führer". Already many people who have been long unemployed are again in positions, workers and soldiers have had wonderful visits to Germany, and this week we are able to use German as well as Austrian stamps, and at last the postage has been reduced...German soldiers and police, and S.S. and S.A. men have contributed much to make us feel that we are no longer Austria but Germany.[8]

Not surprisingly, she decided that she wanted to return home at the end of the year and hoped that the AFSC would be able to find a "permanent mature man Friend soon and not wait till September". In the meantime, an experienced British relief worker, Ethel Haughton, who had been in Austria during the famine and had helped in the 1934 crisis as well, came to assist her, and in June, Robert Yarnell,[9] a Friend from Philadelphia, arrived with his wife and urged Emma to take a rest, as everyone was afraid that she would break down under the strain.

In July, the Centre was asked to define its status and register as a *Verein*, a term which is difficult to translate but which covers all kinds of clubs and organisations. The authorities wanted to keep records of the membership of the Clubs held at the Centre and decide whether they should be allowed to continue. Robert Yarnell and Emma Cadbury declared in a written statement that they were running the Centre on behalf of the Quakers in America and that it was entirely a philanthropic organisation and therefore no *Verein*.[10] Here they took a different stance from that of the Quakers at the Centre in Berlin, who had never registered it with the authorities for relief purposes. The responsibility for the Berlin Centre had always been shared between the foreign Friends and the Yearly Meeting, but the names of the foreign Friends, Corder Catchpool and Gilbert MacMaster, were removed from its letterhead shortly after Hitler came to power in 1933, so that later the German Quakers could suggest to the Nazis that they had "no international links or dependency on Quakerism in England, even though the Society had first been established there. Our Quaker roots lie in German mysticism".[11] The Executive Committee of the Yearly Meeting also issued a declaration that the Society of Friends was no peace organisation, no charitable or humanitarian federation of any kind but a purely religious society.[12] When the German Emergency Committee in London sent William Hughes to Germany for twelve months in October 1933 to give assistance to all those suffering hardship and persecution under the new rulers, he did not work from the Berlin Centre but interviewed people in their homes or in cafés. And when the Friends in Philadelphia wanted to send "ample funds" for relief work in view of the worsening situation in the autumn of 1938, the German Friends who were consulted about using the Centre for such work were "far from enthusiastic".[13] They wanted to guard against a "prejudice of essential Quaker Centre activities through an overburdening of relief work".[14]

In Vienna, on the other hand, there had been no Viennese Friend on the Centre Committee since Rudolf Böck's death in 1927, and so it was felt that there was no need to consult the Viennese Friends when it was decided to use the Vienna Centre for relief purposes only. As there were even more people in need of help in Vienna than in Berlin, the funds from the USA could be put to good use there.

In trying to get recognition of the right of Jewish emigrants to take at least some of their property with them when they left the country, Robert Yarnell explained in a statement to the Ministry of Trade in Berlin on 22 July that he was motivated by a sense of justice which caused him to reject any kind of exaggerated and unnecessary cruelty towards any people whatsoever.[15] His attempts to get better conditions for the emigrants were doomed to failure. Hitler's policy was to use the intimidation of the Jews, the removal of all their rights and the confiscation of their property as a sign to the rest of the population that any attempt to resist would only lead to further repression. In private conversation with trusted Nazis, he explained that through the treatment of the Jews, the rest of the population could be subdued:

> The masses are given a demonstration of the fact that legal guarantees and concepts of property and order are helpless in the face of violence.[16]

As soon as the *Gestapo* entered Austria, they began confiscating Jewish property. Any Jew who possessed more than 5000 Mark had to declare it to the authorities. Those who wanted to emigrate had to pay so many taxes that nothing was left of their money. Nevertheless, to the outside world, Hitler was anxious to maintain a semblance of legality. In taking over more than ninety Austrian banks, eighty-five of which were in Jewish hands, the Nazis gave the impression that they were only interested in reconstructing the banking system in order to make it more efficient. Before closing down the Austrian National Bank, the Nazis moved all the reserves to the German Reichsbank. It was a huge amount, including about 150kg of gold bullion, worth 350,000,000 German Marks, as Austria, unlike Germany, had concentrated on stabilising the currency. The total spoil for that year, including the sale of foreign currency, foreign stocks and shares, more gold deposited in the Bank of England, gold coins etc., amounted to nearly four times that amount. As a result of acquiring all this wealth, Germany was able to spend three times as much on armaments in 1938 as it had done the previous year.[17] The Nazis then turned to confiscating the private property of those considered to be enemies of the regime.

Reluctantly, in the face of the growing threats to her many friends, Emma Cadbury allowed herself to be persuaded to take a three-week holiday, but she was unable to forget the many people who were depending on her to get them out of Austria and so she decided to spend part of her "holiday" at a conference in Evian, which had been called by the American President, Roosevelt, to discuss what could be done to help Jewish refugees.

On the border between France and Germany, she had a frightening experience, when she was stripped and searched by border guards, and one of the letters she was carrying with her to post outside Germany was confiscated. She was probably right in thinking that the search was meant to intimidate her as an American rather than to find anything of importance, since the guards did not even open her suitcase and rucksack.[18]

In Evian, she met Mary Ormerod, who was a co-ordinator for the refugee work of the Friends German Emergency Committee in London. They soon found that it was difficult to convince people that there were other people as well as the religious Jews who were in danger.[19] The Jewish agencies determined who was Jewish by their affiliation to the Jewish *Kultusgemeinde* and by whether or not their mothers were Jewish. Altogether it was estimated that there were under 200,000 Jews in Austria, most of them concentrated in the capital. The Nazi definition of who was to be regarded as "non-Aryan", on the other hand, included all those with Jewish ancestry, whatever their religion. According to Emma Cadbury's estimate, this category included about 60,000 Austrian Catholics and another 10,000 Protestants, as well as several thousand who belonged to no denomination, among them many Socialists and Freemasons. All of them were likely to be persecuted.[20]

She realised that nothing very definite could be expected from the conference and that the delegates could not promise very much on the part of their various governments. The difficulties caused by the fact that the emigrants were not allowed to take much, if any, of their money with them were frequently mentioned. Emigrants from Austria were allowed to take even less than those from Germany. They were not allowed to take more than 10 Mark in German money, which was the equivalent of just less than one pound,[21] and the equivalent of 20 Mark in foreign currency. Many were released from prison on condition that they handed over all their property and left the country within a few weeks. Emma Cadbury was forced to the conclusion that nothing could be done but to comply with such demands:

> It appears to me that the persecution in various forms is intended to hasten their departure, whether by humiliating them with cleaning pavements or barracks - a method which seems to be no longer pursued - or by ruining their businesses by signs on the window or picketing the stores, or by forcing them to sell or at least to give over the business to a commissioner who may be quite incompetent; or the more recent method of wholesale imprisonment and then a demand to leave within a definite time. This has brought much pressure on consulates to hasten the issuance of visas, within the possibilities of their laws and regulations. I have had very little evidence of personal violence. But the moral pressure is very strong...The kindest thing we can do is to help them to do what the party wants them to do.[22]

By July, the Centre had the names of over 1000 people who wanted to escape registered on its lists, and more were flocking in every day, as the repressive measures against all those felt to be opposed to the regime, especially the Jews, increased. When the Friends analysed the cases according to religion, they found that a third of them were Catholics. Some of them were found to be on several lists belonging to different organisations, so that sometimes an individual ended up with more than one affidavit allowing him to leave, but the precious documents, which could have saved the lives of others on the lists, were not transferable and had to be wasted. In order to avoid such duplication, the Friends decided to concentrate on those people who had no other organisation to turn to. The *Kultusgemeinde* helped only its own members, the Catholics were advised to go to their own relief organisation, whereas the Protestants were helped by a Swedish Lutheran church. Another organisation run by a Dutchman, Frank van Gheel-Gildermeester, also helped some of the Jews to emigrate, but he was not trusted by all of them because he had

had close dealings with the Nazis in the past. Although the work was divided up in this way, more people came to the Centre each day than the personnel there could deal with.

One privilege granted to the Quakers which was not allowed to the other welfare organisations was that the authorities did not insist on seeing their records. On one occasion, two Gestapo officials did come to the office and demanded access to the books, but, according to Ethel Haughton, "an appeal to the authorities relieved us of their unwelcome attentions".[23]

Whereas in Germany the restrictions on the Jewish communities were introduced gradually over a number of years, in Vienna they struck immediately and with full force. On 1st July, practically all Jews were dismissed from their employment without notice, and those living in municipal flats were told they had to leave. Even in private houses they were not safe, since they could be turned out of their flats if there were any so-called Aryans living in the house, even if the house had a Jewish owner. Pensions were cancelled, and many were faced with complete destitution. The situation was so desperate that Ethel Haughton and Käthe Neumayer felt it was necessary to start organising food parcels for them straight away, without waiting for the return of Emma Cadbury. They wrote to Friends House in London, begging for financial help. [24]

The enormity of the problem must have been quite clear to them by this time, as well as the great personal risk they were running, especially Käthe Neumayer, who had no foreign Embassy to protect her and no chance of leaving the country, should she fall foul of the authorities.

With the permission of the Gestapo and in co-operation with the *Kultusgemeinde*, Mary Campbell used the experience she had gained in Marienthal to set up a training camp in Kagran, a district on the outskirts of Vienna, where some of those hoping to get out of Austria could be trained in basic agricultural and gardening skills. The participants thought that they might be able to go as a group to some country which still needed agricultural workers, possibly to South America, as they realised that things were tightening up and it would be very difficult to get visas for a European country. Many of them were professional people, doctors and lawyers, who had never done any manual work before. There were also some young people, still almost children, who were able to forget for a time the danger they were in. The camp rescued them from their terrible isolation, so that they were able to enjoy singing and working together. Almost sixty years later, one of them described this experience as the happiest time of her life.[25] She and her young companions were not aware of the harassment experienced by the organisers of the camp. Sometimes they were not able to go on with the project because the Gestapo put

Jewish doctors learning to do manual work at the Quaker workcamp in Kagran in preparation for emigration to South America. August 1938.
(RUTH KARRACH)

various difficulties in their way, such as cutting off the water that they needed for the gardens.[26]

In England, Helen Andrews, who had been in charge of the Agricultural Department of the Centre in the days when the Friends brought cows to Austria to feed the starving children, worked to get permission for this group to go to England to complete their training before going on to South America. Arrangements were made for them to go to various training centres, including the Bruderhof community in Gloucestershire. There were by this time 140 of them, as well as 32 children. The German Committee in London guaranteed their upkeep and training in England, and the Vienna workers started preparing their papers. The first of this group, 52 emigrants, left for England in September 1938; the others were to follow later. They were admitted to England as "transmigrants undergoing training". Eighteen of the children were sent to the Quaker school at Omenn in Holland, which had been opened in April 1934 to provide education and shelter for those children who had to flee from Nazi Germany.[27] Not many of the group actually reached South America, since their enthusiasm for life on the land waned once they got to England. Helen Andrews had great difficulty in getting them to go on with the training and was upset because their refusal put the

Quakers in a quandary, as the refugees had signed an agreement that they would soon move on. They now argued that the signature had been given under duress. Eventually, a former lawyer agreed to keep to the agreement, and the rest followed his lead.[28] The outbreak of war meant that most of them were allowed to stay in England or Ireland, and many were able to return to their original professions.

Between Hitler's annexation of Austria and the outbreak of war in September 1939, thousands of applications for help with emigration from individuals and families were dealt with. The Friends had to try to find guarantees abroad for all of the would-be emigrants. On receiving the *affidavits*, they had to prepare emigration papers for them. From April 1939, guarantors in Britain had to deposit fifty pounds for each of the would-be immigrants.[29] The sources give different figures for the total of those whom the Quakers helped to get to safety before war broke out; they vary between 2,408 and 4,500.[30] How much work this entailed for Emma Cadbury and her small staff can be estimated when one reads how many documents each of the emigrants needed to submit to the *Zentralstelle für Jüdische Auswanderung* (Central Office for Jewish Emigration), which Adolf Eichmann had opened in the former Rothschild palace in August 1938. Finding sufficient funding for all the people who wanted to emigrate remained a central problem, much of the money coming from Quaker organisations in the USA.

In spite of all this overwork, Emma Cadbury managed to maintain an atmosphere of calm efficiency, so that "the Friends' Centre was like a small island of peace and sanity in the middle of the city, which seemed like a mad and stormy sea".[31] She listened to all those who turned to her for help and used whatever knowledge and influence she had to alleviate the sufferings of those who were in prison or turned out of their homes.

Hilda Clark returned to Vienna once more, this time in her capacity of Honorary Secretary of the German Emergency Committee, which was formed by the Quakers in London in October 1938 to help with the increasing number of those desperate to escape from the Nazis. She interviewed people who were on the Quaker lists, trying to fit the applicants to the openings for them in Britain, a heartbreaking task when it came to deciding which of them to choose and which had to be rejected. Yet she was never one to run away from difficulties. It must have been especially hard for her to be reminded of the fact that the children she had saved from the famine were now young adults, once more trapped into a tragic situation and facing one another as persecutors or victims. She then went back to London to supervise the rescue work from that end. One of her fellow workers paid tribute to her work there:

Only those most closely concerned can know what the work owed at this stage of rapid expansion to the steady faith and practical experience of Hilda Clark.[32]

In September, the Yarnells sailed for the USA, taking some of Emma Cadbury's luggage with them. She herself could not decide to leave Vienna until somebody had been found to replace her. In the middle of October, several Friends arrived from England to assist her, and after deciding that they were all suitable for the task, she started making definite plans for her journey. Ethel Haughton was to take over the general administration of the Centre in her place. All of the new arrivals were dedicated Quakers, who were interested in supporting the Vienna Meeting as well as carrying on with the emigration work.[33] Feeling that she was leaving the office in good hands, Emma Cadbury was able to make arrangements to sail to USA in time for Christmas, travelling through London to attend London Yearly Meeting and staying for a few days with Elisabeth Horsenaill to console her on the death of her husband.[34]

Meanwhile, in Vienna the situation had worsened still further. After the pogrom of the so-called *Kristallnacht* on the night of 9th-10th November, during which Jewish synagogues were burned, shops plundered and over 6000 Jews were taken into custody, more and more restrictions were put on the Jewish population, fines were imposed, and they became increasingly impoverished.

One of the secretaries of the Friends' German Emergency Committee in London, Bertha Bracey, shocked by the news from Germany, went with the Liberal statesman, Lord Samuel, to persuade the Home Secretary to secure permission from Parliament to allow Jewish children into Britain. On receiving the promise of visas to enter Britain for ten thousand children between the ages of three months and seventeen years, a small group of Friends went to Vienna to make the arrangements, as it was felt to be too dangerous for British Jews to travel there.[35] The Vienna Centre was plunged into feverish activity, trying to get as many children as possible out of danger, even though it meant they had to travel without their parents. Those children were given priority whose circumstances were particularly difficult because their parents were already in prison or had been forced to flee. Before the outbreak of war put an end to this activity, the Quakers alone enabled 1200 children to leave Austria. Not only Britain but also Holland and Sweden admitted large numbers of children.[36]

About thirty children were sent to a school in Montmorency near Paris, run by an Austrian Socialist, Ernst Papanek, himself a refugee from the Nazis. Many of them were still so terrified by what they had gone through that they were unable to speak for several weeks. The assistants at the school saw it as their main task to restore the children's confidence and help them to recover from their traumatic experiences. Quaker relief workers in France supported them and took over the care of those children who had to be hospitalised. Papanek later paid tribute to their work and the spirit in which it was carried out. He saw the strength of the Quakers in the fact that they did not take sides and they helped anyone who was in need. He himself had witnessed in Vienna how the oppressed often become oppressors in their turn, and he thought that the Quakers' impartiality enabled them to influence the Nazis in situations in which others were regarded with mistrust. While the Quakers did manage to save the lives of one or two of these children, the majority later fell into the hands of the Gestapo and their French counterparts and were sent to Auschwitz.[37]

Many of those children who were sent to England have since told the story of their lives before and after their sad journey. In their accounts, relief at having escaped and gratitude towards those who had saved them are mixed with guilt at having left their families to their fate and resentment at the unimaginative treatment that some of them received on their arrival in England.[38] Confused and unhappy, unable to comprehend what was happening to them, some had difficulty in adapting to their new lives, and their misery was often interpreted as ingratitude.

Ruth Karrach, for example, the girl who had so much enjoyed the training camp in Kagran, was accompanied to England by a Quaker English teacher, who offered to take Ruth's beloved mandolin, as the children were not allowed to take any of their belongings with them. She also arranged for Ruth to become a pupil at the school where she taught. Each day, Ruth had to stand before the whole school at assembly and say some words which were drilled into her, without understanding what she was saying. As her English improved, she realised that she was thanking the other pupils for the pennies they contributed each day to pay her fees at the school. No-one seemed to notice her sense of humiliation and her extreme unhappiness. Her Jewish father had escaped to Belgium, whereas her mother had gone to Turkey, hoping that he would be able to join her there, but he disappeared into the concentration camps when the Germans invaded Belgium. How could Ruth's fellow pupils be expected to understand why she did not seem to appreciate their efforts on her behalf?[39]

The Centre still had 650 children who were waiting to get away from Vienna on its lists when the outbreak of war forced the British workers to leave and the escape route was closed.

NOTES

[1] Emma Cadbury to her family 12th March 1938: HCSC.
[2] Headley Horsenaill, the representative of the London Friends' Service Council, who had been such a stabilising force since he first came to

Ruth Karrach's passport, issued to enable her to leave Austria with the Kindertransport (RUTH KARRACH)

Vienna in 1922, had been forced to resign in September 1937 because of ill health, caused by a burst ulcer which had poisoned his whole system. He had been under considerable stress for several years. See report from the Vienna Centre: January 15th, 1938.

[3] Rudi Böck to Alice Nike 13th November 1937.

[4] Mary Campbell to Alice Nike 19th July 1938. FHL.

[5] "Dieses Ja ist aufrichtiger Dank an den gnädigen Gott für Rettung und Befreiung unserer Heimat" quoted in Botz 1988: 126. My translation in text.

[6] What the reasons for Renner's declaration were has never been fully explained. Some evidence seems to show that he hoped to save other leading socialists or threatened members of his family from the concentration camp. Botz:140ff.

[7] For a detailed analysis of the result of the plebiscite and the reasons for it see: Botz 1988: 151ff.

[8] Emma Cadbury to her family 6th April 1938: HCSC.

[9] Robert Yarnell had been in charge of the child-feeding programme in Germany from 1923-24.

[10] Correspondence between the Friends International Centre and the *Reichskommissar für die Wiedervereinuigung Österreichs mit dem Deutschen Reich* 29th June and 1 July 1938: Austrian Staatsarchiv.

[11] Hans Albrecht to Regierungsrat Hagenbruch at the Gestapo headquarters in Berlin: 7th August 1942; quoted in Bailey 1994: 151.

[12] Quoted in Otto 1972: 197.

[13] Article by Roger Carter on *The Quaker International Centre in Berlin, 1920-42* in *The Journal of the Friends' Historical Society Vol.56 No.1.*

[14] Minutes of the Internationales Sekretariat, Berlin, held at Stettin 8th July 1938. Hans Albrecht drew the attention of Howard and Katherine Elkington and Roger Carter to a Minute to this effect from the Executive Committee. FHL/GE.

[15] Rosenkranz 1978: 191.

[16] Rauschnig 1939: 97.

[17] The figures are given in a brochure produced to accompany an exhibition *Wien 1938* in the Historical Museum in Vienna 1 March - 30 June 1988.

[18] Emma Cadbury to her family 12th July 1938: HCSC.

[19] Corder Catchpool to Bertha Bracey 4th November 1935. FSC/GE5. FHL.
As Corder Catchpool explained to the London Friends, there was confusion even in Germany about who should be considered "non-Aryan". The term was a racial one according to the Nazi authorities, whereas the definition by the Jewish agencies of who was Jewish was based on religious criteria. 4,900 Viennese who were not Jews according to the

Nazi's racial definition were more or less forced to leave the *Kultusgemeinde*, that is, the Jewish religious community.

[20] Emma Cadbury to her family 12th July 1938.
The Viennese *Dokumentationsarchiv des österreichischen Widerstandes*, a trustworthy source, gives the total number of those who did not adhere to the Jewish religion but were classified as Jews by the Nazis as 24,000. Probably Emma Cadbury's figures also include those classified as *Mischlinge*, a derogatory term to denote anyone who had fewer than three Jewish grandparents. They were often not members of the Jewish community. Although they were not in quite the same danger as the first category, they were subjected to humiliation and degradation, and their future prospects were bleak

[21] What this sum represented can perhaps be assessed by remembering that a British labourer at the time earned about three pounds a week.

[22] ibid.

[23] Darton 1954: 46.

[24] Ethel Haughton and Käthe Neumayer to Alice Nike: 9th July 1938.

[25] Interview with Ruth Karrach 1997.

[26] Rosenkranz H. !978: 193.

[27] Hoxie Jones 1937 347.

[28] Darton 1954: 48ff.

[29] ibid.

[30] According to the British historian J. Ormerod Greenwood, "between March 1938 and the outbreak of war, the office of the old Baroque palace in the Singerstrasse handled 11,000 applications affecting 15,000 people, prepared detailed case papers for 8,000 families and single persons, and got 4,500 individuals away to many countries, each of which had its different immigration procedures" (Greenwood 1975: 267). The American Professor Hans Schmitt, on the other hand, says, "According to the meticulous statistics that survive, 6,000 cases, representing 13,745 persons, were registered between March 15, 1938, and August 28, 1939, and 2,408 of this total were ultimately able to leave. They included 1,588 men, 509 women, and 311 dependants, the largest number, 1,264 going to England, 165 to the United States, and 107 to Australia. (Schmitt 1997:163). The discrepancies are probably largely due to the fact that Greenwood's figures include the children who travelled to England on the *Kindertransporte* (see p.102 below)

[31] Quoted from an unpublished manuscript by Phyllis M. Richards, who turned to Emma Cadbury for help in rescuing a elderly woman from the clutches of the Gestapo in 1938 and enabling her and her small grandson to escape to England.

[32] Quoted in Darton 1954: 52.

[33] Emma Cadbury to her family 19th October: HCSC.

[34] Emma Cadbury to her sister 23rd November: HCSC.

[35] Leverton & Löwensohn 1990: 377.
[36] Ethel Haughton to Alice Nike: 6th December 1938. FHL.
[37] Papanek 1980: 143.
[38] Altogether more than ten thousand children were taken to safety, most of them from the lists of the Jewish *Kultusgemeinde*. For the stories of many of these children see Leverton B & Löwensohn S *I came alone: the story of the Kindertransports* The Book Guild, London 1990.
[39] Interview with Ruth Karrach: 1997.

CHAPTER 11

Conscience and Confusion

IN JANUARY 1939, when Bernard Lawson went to Vienna once more, it was to find that the Vienna Group had carried out many of the recommendations he had made on the occasion of his last visit in 1937. They had become members of the German Yearly Meeting immediately after the *Anschluss*, when it looked as if Austria had lost its independence for ever. Thus they came under the leadership of the German clerk, Hans Albrecht. They had also become almost completely independent of the Vienna Centre and now held their Meeting for Worship in one of their homes on Wednesday evenings rather than attending the Sunday Meeting at the Centre.

But the circumstances which had compelled these changes were not those which Bernard Lawson had envisaged on his previous visit. Since the preceding March, the attendance at the Sunday Meeting at the Centre had been rising steadily until it reached an average of about 60, but most of the attenders knew very little about Quakerism, as Mary Campbell reported:

> Of these only three or four are usually members of the group and many others are there for the first time and have absolutely no knowledge of the meaning of Quakerism or the form of worship. As these newcomers have come to us for a variety of reasons, not least among them material help, it is a very big task to tackle the really earnest seekers that are among them.[1]

Bernard Lawson went to the Meeting for Worship on Sunday morning to see for himself, and afterwards he wrote:

> The Vienna Meeting was paradoxical - larger than it had ever been (65 present on the Sunday I was there) but hardly any of the actual members present. It was foreign friends who were giving the most support. Partly this was due to the very busy lives of the few members but also to the political situation, particularly as regards Jews, who made up a large proportion of the meeting.[2]

The Centre was rapidly becoming one of the few places in Vienna where Jewish people were welcomed. To encourage those among them who showed a real interest in Quakerism, the Friends started a Study Circle once a week, which was usually attended by about 12 people, most of whom were planning to leave the country as soon as possible.[3]

Because they feared that the Gestapo would take note of any Austrians who frequented the Centre, the members of the Forum Club had completely severed their connections with it in rather upsetting circumstances. It was no longer possible to organize regular Club evenings at the Centre, but the foreign Friends had suggested to Riki Teller,[4] who had been the leader of the Club for many years, that she ought to maintain some kind of contact with its members and perhaps invite them in small groups to the Centre.[1] She did invite several of them, but they told her that they would prefer not to come to the Centre at all, as owing to the Friends' emigration work, they were "apt to have a number of non-Aryans on the premises".[2] Riki had to write a long letter to London, explaining that it was becoming too difficult to run the Club, particularly as the Forum Committee had suggested that they should keep to the Nüremberg Laws and exclude "non-Aryans":

> Of the three full Jewish members, two resigned, apparently voluntarily, but the third has been told by one of the other members that he cannot attend the Club, and since then has been absent.. he was one of the keenest and nicest members...[3]

In her letter, Riki tried to excuse the Forum Committee by pointing out that, if the Club were to remain open to Jewish members, the others would be afraid to come to the Club meetings, even if they were held away from the Centre:

> All public officials or those who want to be, who are paid by the State or municipality (teachers, lawyers, doctors etc) as well as all members of the *NSDAP* (the National Socialist Workers' Party of Germany) and its branches, will not be able to come. Also "half-Jews" who are kept on in State positions as teachers etc would keep away. Only the "full Jewish" people would remain.
>
> The purpose of the Club is lost, and it has no sense to keep it on...A great political change, like the one we have now lived through, affects everyone, and there is hardly any one of the group - which was, as you know, a purely intellectual one - who has not been affected by Austria joining with Germany.[4]

She also reminded the London Friends that several of the members were hoping for employment for the first time in their lives and were afraid of jeopardizing their chances by associating with Jews. Some were going to Germany, some, who had found work in Vienna, were so busy that they no longer had any interest in coming to the Club, while others, presumably the Jewish members and perhaps others who felt themselves threatened, were planning to leave for England, France or "oversea States"(*sic*).

On the other hand, Riki Teller did realize that it would be against the whole Quaker ethic to exclude Jews, so she proposed giving up the Club altogether and perhaps trying to keep in touch with some of the members by letter. However, soon afterwards she went to Germany to join her husband, who had taken up the offer of employment there, and with her departure, the Centre lost all contact with the members of the Forum Club. Thus, all the efforts made by the Centre for so many years to bring together young people from different backgrounds and with different convictions and to teach them tolerance and respect for one another came to nothing.

The ties of friendship between people of different social, religious and political backgrounds - the "Wider Fellowship", as Emma Cadbury would have called it - which had held during the years of Austro-Fascism under Dollfuss and Schuschnigg did not prove strong enough when subjected to the strain of living under a more ruthless regime. Those who were not in immediate danger of persecution were lured by the prospect of employment to desert their friends when they were most in need of comfort and support.

The discipline of membership and a shared spiritual life seems to have forged stronger links among those belonging to the Vienna Group, which by this time had been reduced to six active members. Katherina Böck, whose warm hospitality had nurtured the group in its early years, had died at Easter 1938, and her sister, another long-standing member, was too old and ill to contribute any more to the life of the Meeting. The former Clerk of the Vienna Group, Ottilie Guttwillinger, had married an Englishman and gone to England to live there permanently. She worked as a secretary to the German committee of the FSC, where her knowledge of conditions in Austria and her links with the Centre must have been invaluable. In one of her letters to Vienna, she enquires about the arrangements for emigration that were being made for Dr Bruno Bettelheim, the renowned child psychologist, and sends a letter from the Home Office to assist him.[5]

Two of the oldest members, Dr Kreisler, who was a well-known lawyer and a highly respected and cultured man, and his wife, both of whom had joined the Society in the early days, were helped to emigrate, as Frau Kreisler was of Jewish descent. Some of the typical dilemmas of many of the emigrants are illustrated by their case. As they had no religious affiliations with the Jewish *Kultusgemeinde* and had not considered themselves to be Jews, they could not look to the Jewish agencies for help. They would like to have gone to England but seem to have had less difficulty in getting the precious affidavit which was required for immigration into the U.S.A., where they had some vague connections. Like many others, they had to grasp at whatever straw they could find. It was doubtful whether Dr Kreisler would be able to get work as a lawyer because of the language difficulties and the specialised legal knowledge required in a strange country, so the Friends in Vienna stressed his wife's accomplishments:

> She is good teacher of singing and voice training and also of German and French and I believe Italian. English Friends think they might be able to find occupation for him also. They would have to be supported here in any case and it probably would not cost much more abroad and they would be much relieved if they could get away.[6]

Although he does not mention the Kreislers by name, probably in order to avoid shaming them, Clarence Pickett describes, in his reminiscences of his time as Executive Secretary of the AFSC, a visit they made to his house in Philadelphia, where they lived for some months while looking for a permanent place:

> It was a good deal of a shock to see them when they came to us - a bewildered father, having lost the chance to pursue his profession, the mother forgetful and continually anxious. She would touch the piano and wander about as though in a constant daze. It was different with the children. The girl was immediately busy in a job as a stenographer. Through her energy and skill she made a place for herself in her new country, married happily, and is a well-adjusted, useful American citizen. The boy quickly perfected his English in American schools, found his way into a job, married a charming American girl, and almost completely escaped any disastrous effects of the transfer.[7]

Especially older people had the greatest difficulties in coping with the abrupt loss of identity and simply could not replace it by the one imposed on them by the Nazi regime. This was particularly true of those who had previously not considered themselves to be Jews. They had no sense of a shared identity with the Jewish community. As one of them wrote, all he had in common with his fellow Jews was "solidarity in the face of threats":

> With Jews as Jews I share practically nothing: no language, no cultural tradition, no childhood memories.[8]

This loss of identity was a terrible affliction imposed on those victimized by the Nazis, whether they managed to flee from Germany or not. It was one of the causes of many suicides, even among those who reached safety. It has not been possible to trace what became of these two members of the Vienna Group. It would be comforting to discover that their

Quaker identity eventually helped them to recover some form of equilibrium in their new home.

Although only one or two of them regularly attended the Sunday Meeting at the Centre, it speaks for the strength of their Quaker convictions that the remaining members of the tiny Vienna Group still met regularly each week for Meeting for Worship in the privacy of their own homes, even though such gatherings were forbidden and could have led to their being denounced to the Gestapo. They also invited the foreign Friends from the Centre to join them. Emma Cadbury met with them regularly until she left Vienna, although she would have preferred them to come to the Centre. All of them probably needed the Meeting for Worship and the sense of continued fellowship to give them strength to face the difficulties of their everyday lives and to help them to hang on to the beliefs and principles which had sustained them through so many trials and tribulations.

Wilhelmine Ottenfeld worked at the Centre in the mornings, trying to keep its difficult finances in order, as well as working in a sugar factory in the afternoons. Like the others at the Centre, she was under dreadful strain, struggling to find an acceptable solution to the difficulties of all those who turned to the Friends for help.

Bernard Lawson was able to see for himself how difficult the work at the Centre had become:

> The Vienna Centre is now practically completely absorbed in relief work of one kind or another. The Clubs have entirely ceased - not even a "shadow" club remains - also the Adult School and the Friends' International Service Union... The Centre is filled every day with crowds of enquirers, or parents wishing to send their children to England, but it is well organised and the interviews divided out systematically...The situation therefore is completely different from Berlin and, by contrast, the latter office (*Berlin*) was peaceful - maybe the most outwardly normal of our European Centres at present.[9]

In the first few days after the annexation of Austria, thousands of Socialists, as well as Christian Socialist leaders and Communists, had been arrested by the Gestapo. The exact numbers are hard to define, as many were arrested without any warrant, and some were released after a few days. It is estimated that altogether about 70,000 were arrested, between 10,000 and 20,000 people being kept in prison for a longer period,[10] and several hundreds being sent to the concentration camp in Dachau. A system of spies and denunciators was built up so that anyone who was thought to be hostile to the regime might be arrested. Pacifists were as much hated and despised as Communists, as to Hitler they were objects of the deepest contempt.[11]

Of the small Vienna Group, Alois Jalkotzy, especially, must have felt himself to be in a very dangerous position, not only as a leading Socialist but also as a member of an organisation, the Religious Society of Friends, which was known for its pacifist attitudes. In fact, he was arrested twice and held for questioning by the Gestapo.[5]

The foreign Friends were shocked to hear that Rudi Böck, who was now the Clerk of the Vienna Group, had become enthusiastic about the Nazi leadership. Perhaps, by 1939 most of them had forgotten that several of their own political leaders, as well as other well-known figures, had been impressed by Hitler at one point. As the Viennese-born, distinguished journalist, Gitta Sereny writes:

> This was the time people now like to forget, when American expatriate writer Gertrude Stein thought Hitler should get the Nobel Peace prize; George Bernard Shaw passionately defended him: the Swedish explorer Sven Hedin lauded his "indomitable passion for justice, breadth of political vision, unerring foresight and a genuine solicitude for the welfare of his fellow citizens"; and Britons such as Lord Halifax (in reports to the Foreign Office) and David Lloyd George conferred their stamp of approval. "Hitler is a born leader of men, a dynamic personality with resolute will and a dauntless heart, who is trusted by the old and idolised by the young," wrote Lloyd George in the *Daily Express* after attending the 1936 Olympics".[12]

Even Churchill is quoted as saying that he hoped that "Great Britain would have a man like Hitler in times of peril".[13]

With the wisdom of hindsight, knowing as we do of the terrible suffering that Hitler brought upon the world, with the deaths of millions of people in the most dreadful circumstances, it is difficult to put ourselves into the frame of mind of people who, at the time, could not foresee the extent of the coming disaster. Most of those who greeted Hitler's troops in Austria with cheering and delight were not cheering the persecution of the Jews or the likelihood of war. They were hoping for an end to unemployment and to the uncertainty about Austria's future that had overshadowed them since the break-up of the Empire. Many who had hated the *Ständestaat* also cheered the downfall of Schuschnigg's government, which was the worst form of repression they had experienced up to then.

At first their hopes seemed justified:

> Although they persecuted leading Socialists as well as prominent Catholic supporters of Schuschnigg and Jews, in the first few days after the invasion of Austria by Hitler's troops, the National

Socialists gave back their old jobs to many of the Socialists who had been excluded from work since the uprising in 1934. Others who had been excluded from unemployment benefits and were completely destitute now received the same unemployment payments as the other unemployed. They received food packets and the promise of work in the near future, so that many of the Socialists were enthusiastic about the new regime, at least at the beginning. Their attitude changed in 1939 after the outbreak of war, when people remembered the old socialist parole, "Fascism means war".[14]

Rudi Böck soon had a special motive for supporting the new regime. As a civil servant, working as an architect for the Vienna Town Council, Rudi Böck would, like all the other civil servants, have had to swear loyalty to the new regime. There is no record of anyone refusing to take this oath, although there were many opponents of the new regime within the ranks of the civil servants, including many Jews. Perhaps Rudi Böck ought to have remembered the early Quakers and their injunctions against oaths, but swearing loyalty to the State was so common in Austria that it would have been impossible to hold public office of any kind without doing so.[6] It must have been a relief to Rudi Böck when, on 13th March, the day after the annexation of Austria, a man already well-known to him and the other Quakers in Vienna was installed as the new *Bürgermeister* (Lord Mayor). In the twenties and early thirties, Hermann Neubacher had been director of the GESIBA, the municipal department which had organised the Land Settlements, the housing scheme so dear to Rudi Böck's heart. After the Socialists lost control of the Municipal Council when they were outlawed in 1934, the housing situation in Vienna had deteriorated once more, as very few houses were built under their successors. Immediately after taking office, Neubacher promised to remedy the situation and began making plans to extend the boundaries of the city so as to provide more building space. He asked for suggestions for a new era of building, in which the idea of Land Settlements would once more play a central role. He also published articles in several newspapers, advocating a revival of the "cottage settlement" idea and describing its philosophical basis in terms similar to those used by the Quakers in the early twenties.[15]

Rudi Böck became one of the "inner planning committee of engineers and architects" responsible for designing the enlargement of the city in accordance with these ideas.[7] It must have seemed as if his dreams were at last coming true, and he no doubt envisaged for himself an important position in planning the city of the future. Many Austrians were convinced that their beloved city would now be restored to its old beauty and importance, especially as Hitler promised that he would "give Vienna the setting which such a pearl deserved".[16] They did not know of Hitler's determination to break the cultural dominance of Vienna and build up the importance of Linz and Graz instead. It was to be turned into a provincial town which would never be allowed to rival Berlin.

Rudi Böck must have talked about such plans for erecting new Settlements when he tried to explain his new enthusiasm for the Nazis to British and American Friends. One of them, a young American, Leonard Kenworthy, who worked at the Berlin Centre in 1940, wrote scornfully after the war, "He seemed to think he was going to become a new William Penn".[17] At the time, however, such ideas were taken seriously, and there were numerous articles in the leading newspapers, with such headlines as "Vienna: the beginning of a new era in the Southeast".[18]

One of Emma Cadbury's visitors, Florence Barrow, a Birmingham Friend who had been head of the Quaker mission in Poland, describes how she went with other workers from the Centre to talk to Bürgermeister Neubacher about the plans of the Friends for helping the "non-Aryan Christians (*sic*)" and to elicit his help in proposing these ideas to the Gestapo:

> The Bürgermeister, who had known the Friends' work for many years, was very sympathetic and considered the Gestapo unreasonable in thinking that Jewish funds should provide for non-Aryan Christians. He was concerned, too, with the need which exists among them. He promised to have an interview with Herr Bürkel (*sic*) himself, and to consult him as to the proposed scheme for Friends helping by food vouchers and in other ways. (No reply had come before I left).[19]

There seems to be no record that a reply ever was received, and one might be tempted to dismiss Neubacher's promise as yet another of the attempts by the National Socialists to lull people into believing that they were not as bad as their reputation, except that Bürckel, who, first as *Reichskommissar* and then as *Gauleiter*, was directly responsible to Hitler for transferring the whole organisation of the country into the hands of the National Socialists, later charged Neubacher with being too friendly with the Jews and used it as an excuse for getting him removed from his post. Neubacher had certainly employed many Jews in his municipal department, and he seems to have believed that the persecution would die down, once the "revolutionary phase" had passed. On the 17th March 1938, he wrote in the leading Austrian newspaper:

> When the days of ferment are over, and they are already fading away, Vienna must become a showcase of Austrian discipline.

He did not realise that he, like all the more moderate Austrian National Socialists, would soon have no more influence on events and that Hitler would never give up his obsession with what was euphemistically referred to as the "Jewish problem".[20]

Rudi Böck, for his part, was anxious to assure the Friends that his new enthusiasm did not mean that he was not concerned about the Jews. Both American and British Friends tried to talk to him and understand his point of view.

Bernard Lawson learned that the Viennese Friends had in mind the possibility of holding a Meeting somewhere else and at a different time, to which they would be prepared to invite a small number of Jews.[21] Their caution was certainly justified, since it would have endangered them all if the gathering had been too large and had come to the notice of the Gestapo. Bernard Lawson passed on a suggestion to the Friends Service Council that they might consider sponsoring a "rightly qualified and experienced German Friend" to organise such a meeting, as the Viennese Friends had neither the time nor the energy to do so alone.[22] He also talked to Hans Albrecht about it, proposing that the German Yearly Meeting should pay a third of the expenses and that the Friend chosen should be prepared to devote about a third of his or her time to the Vienna Group.

In March 1938, when Roger Carter, who had replaced Corder Catchpool as the British representative at the Centre in Berlin, paid another visit to Vienna to consult with the relief workers, he also talked to Rudi Böck, Alois Jalkotzy and the Schindlers, and he, too, reported their reluctance to be associated with the Centre:

> It is not the case that they wish to separate themselves from the type of problem that is cared for in the Centre; on the contrary, each of them is active in a somewhat similar way in spite of the personal danger to themselves. Secondly, they are above all interested in the care of Quakerism as a faith and a way of life, and they feel that this cannot be confused with relief…Thirdly, they feel as a group so shattered by their experiences of the last years that they look first to gaining inward strength and inward cohesion before thinking of group concerns. They have to struggle against difficulties in meeting occasioned by their own very great preoccupation with earning their daily bread and excessively long hours of work.[23]

He realised that the situation was very different from that in Berlin and agreed that the Centre in Vienna should be considered as a relief centre rather than the home of Viennese Quakerism. For the sake of those now turning to the Centre for help, Roger Carter advised that the Meeting for Worship at the Centre should be carried on, "but as a specially Centre concern", and he added:

The separation of the Quaker group and Meeting from the Centre is a pity, but in view of its large-scale relief aspect I think this is inevitable and certainly wise.[24]

Now that the Vienna Friends were part of the German Yearly Meeting, their behaviour was also nervously observed by its Clerk, Hans Albrecht, who decided to send a German Friend to Vienna to give them support, as Bernard Lawson had suggested. The advice that had been given to the members of the German Yearly Meeting by its Executive Committee in April 1933 now also applied to the Viennese Quakers:

> We urge all members, with a full inward sense of responsibility and preparedness, to bear witness to and express the spirit of non-violence, friendship and service wherever they are brought face to face with spiritual or other needs. But we ask them to act with careful restraint and on their own responsibility and not to assume that they must act as Quakers, or could achieve more by acting in the name of Friends than on their own.[8]

On his visit to Europe in September 1938, Clarence Pickett, the Executive Secretary of AFSC, arrived in Vienna, the day before Chamberlain went to Godesberg for his second meeting with Hitler to discuss the fate of Czechoslovakia. A few evenings later, Pickett went to supper with Rudi Böck:

> We were having dinner in an Austrian home, and a number of times during the evening our host excused himself and went to the roof of the house to see whether the planes flying over might be Russian. He was convinced that the USSR had massed thousands of planes just over the Czech border, and they might arrive at any moment.[25]

Had he been able to speak German and communicate better with the people he met, he might have realised that Rudi Böck's fears were shared by many others, and not without reason. Russia and France had guaranteed the independence of Czechoslovakia, which was being violated by Hitler. Not only Austrians but also many Czechs expected the Russians to go to the defence of Czechoslovakia, especially as Russia had not been consulted before the leaders of Britain, Italy and France agreed to let Hitler enter Czechoslovakia and annex the Sudetenland. But the Russians did nothing. The small Czech group of Friends in Prague felt that their country had been betrayed. Two of them died in prison or in a concentration camp.[9]

Clarence Pickett, while generally well informed about Germany, seems to have been unaware of the danger. On the following Sunday, he attended the Meeting at the Centre:

> For many individuals, the chaos of hate, fear and suffering had accentuated the need for periods of quiet, in which they could reunite with others in rediscovering and renewing the inmost sources of calm and strength. I spoke to the Vienna Friends Meeting on Sunday morning, and felt coming to me from the group strangely deep yearnings for words of truth and sincerity, words of comfort and courage. In that hour I wished more than ever that I could speak German. But under such circumstances one's attitude perhaps speaks louder than words.[26]

One imagines that the people at the Meeting were hoping for rather more than comforting words, but Clarence Pickett knew how much resistance the AFSC was meeting in its efforts to persuade the American Government to increase the quota of immigrants it would allow into the United State, so he had not much more to offer them. In the book he wrote later about his work for the AFSC, Pickett describes how desperately the Committee tried to persuade the American authorities to increase the number of Jewish immigrants allowed into the USA, pointing out that the totals for 1938 and 1939 were well under the official quota:

> Our committee encountered strong opposition to the immigration of refugees in 1938 and 1939, the chief reason being fear: the fear that our country would soon be "flooded with refugees", "flooded with Jews" and that the newcomers would swell the ranks of the unemployed, or worse, take jobs from native Americans. Affidavits of support had to be given each refugee before he could immigrate, but this did not mean he was not in some respects a charge on the general resources of the country if he had to be supported by some loyal individual who had become his friend... We discovered that...immigration was in effect limited to 75,000 annually. For the six-year period July 1, 1932 through June 30, 1938, roughly corresponding to the years of the Nazi regime in Germany, 4487 more aliens had departed from than were admitted to the United States...For the year ending 30th June 1938, the year of the largest refugee immigration up to that time, there was a net immigration...for permanent residence of only 42,685.[28]

Robert Yarnell returned to Vienna for two days in December, after a visit to Germany with Rufus Jones, during which they tried, without much success, to get access to leading Nazis and persuade them to modify their treatment of the Jews. He, too, talked to the Clerk of the Vienna Group about his attitude towards the new rulers. He had already observed that "conditions in Austria were very much worse than in the Reich" and he was expecting the Viennese to share his sense of outrage at what was happening to the Jews. Knowing of Rudi Böck's connections with the Nazis, he regarded him as some sort of strange creature; "It's interesting to see and talk to a real, honest, enthusiastic Nazi", he wrote. After listening to Rudi Böck enthusing about the new building plans for Vienna, he decided to ask him about his attitude towards the *Kristallnacht* (night of the broken glass) and the "Jew (*sic*) persecution". According to Yarnell, Rudi Böck answered:

> No, I don't believe in it, but you don't understand the whole thing. November 10th was a spontaneous uprising of the people.

When Yarnell pointed out that there had been similar uprisings against the Jews at the same time in Frankfurt, Berlin and other German cities, so that they could hardly have been spontaneous, Rudi Böck answered:

> Yes, you see, those things must be planned or else they get out of hand.[28]

In the book "Nazis and Quakers" by the American Hans Schmitt, this conversation is interpreted as showing how callous Rudi Böck had become. Professor Schmitt thinks that he must have spoken "without blinking, thinking or blushing".[29] However, all the other details of his life as a Quaker show that Rudi Böck was a highly compassionate man with strong Quaker convictions. It seems more likely that the promise that the Nazis had given that they would help the poor and unemployed, together with his belief that at long last he would be able to follow his calling and provide adequate housing for the poor made him hope, like many other people at the time, that the persecution of the Jews would soon die down. Because he wanted to believe that union with Germany was the best solution to Austria's problems,[10] Böck probably convinced himself that the excesses would never have happened if the authorities in Vienna had been prepared for them beforehand.

This conversation illustrates how hard it is for people to give up beliefs for which they have suffered a lot. According to Leon Festinger's theory of cognitive dissonance, people always seek psychological equilibrium, so that when their beliefs are challenged by counter-information or experience, they tend to overlook or discount conflicting evidence so as to escape from the necessity of having to change their belief system. They claim that it is the facts which may require explanation rather than the beliefs which need to be changed.[30] It seems to have been this mechanism which made Rudi Böck accept Goebbels' version of the *Kristallnacht* as a "spontaneous uprising" rather than admitting that it must have been planned. Had he faced the truth, he would have been forced to share Yarnell's horror and revulsion and revise his allegiance to the Nazi leadership. This, in turn, would have meant having to give up the conviction that he had held for years, that he had been called by God to carry out a special task. It was in answer to this call that he had struggled through many years of poverty to complete his studies as an architect, and he seemed to be so near his goal!

It should also be remembered that Rudi Böck, like so many of his generation in Vienna, had faced poverty and frustration since his early childhood. As a young boy during the famine after the first world war, he had been sent to Switzerland to escape starvation. His early membership of the Society of Friends must have meant isolation and considerable discrimination,[11] for which he probably compensated by developing a feeling of pride in the accomplishments of the Socialists and the Quakers in building up new social structures through child welfare, education and better housing for the workers.. The destruction of much of this work in 1934 must have been a terrible blow to him. The repressive Austro-fascist government under Dollfuss and Schuschnigg, while not as ruthless as the Nazi regime in Germany, had put an end to Socialist hopes for a better future. It also made it very difficult for all those who did not belong to an established church to obtain employment. They were even excluded from higher education, so that many people joined one of the main churches, not from conviction but in order to avoid such discrimination.[12]

Because he was a Quaker and therefore not a member of a recognised church, Rudi Böck must have had difficulty in completing his studies and in finding a suitable post. In Marienthal, while he was trying to alleviate some of the suffering among the unemployed there in 1935, he told one of the British students that he had been waiting for ten years to be able to get married because he could not afford to keep a wife and family. His hard-won independence and the safety of his family would have been jeopardised if he had allowed himself to doubt the validity of the Nazi promises.

While the conviction of being led to take on a particular concern often enabled Quakers to perform acts of bravery and compassion which went far beyond what is normally expected of human beings, as has been illustrated in the accounts of the relief work, the belief that God had a special mission for them sometimes caused them to ignore aspects of the situation which did not fit in with this idea. Rufus Jones, talking of those who have mystical experiences, warned that "the individuals who have these experiences feel themselves divinely "chosen" for a peculiar mission. The startling event marks a sharp break with the old life. And these aspects are apt to produce a remarkable shift of level in such an individual's life. But psychologically such experiences fall into the class of well-known phenomena. They are no more "supernatural" than are the more ordinary and normal experiences of life".[31]

Whatever the original experience, the conviction that he had been chosen to carry the Settlement idea on to its proper conclusion dominated the whole of Rudi Böck's life. He was duped by the Nazis, who had got no further than drawing up plans for extending Vienna's boundaries to provide more land for the scheme when the outbreak of war put an stop to it all. Of the 60,000 new flats that had been promised, only 3,000 were actually built. However, in the end, he did partly achieve his aim. Under a new Socialist municipal council after the war, when Vienna was in ruins, he was put in charge of the department responsible for the restoration of old buildings and for the Settlements. He also remained a Quaker, although he stopped attending Meeting for Worship after a Swedish Friend reproached him for his "Nazi past".[13]

In 1938, it must have seemed to all the Viennese Friends as if there was no alternative to the new government and as if Austria had ceased to exist as an independent country. Unless they came under the Nüremberg Laws like the Kreislers, they were advised by the Friends in England and America to stay in their country and do what they could to improve the situation. At the Friends' World Conference in Swarthmore in 1937, which Rudi Böck attended, together with the Clerk of the German Yearly Meeting, Hans Albrecht, he had heard Friends say:

> We must make an effort to make governments good, rather than merely voice objections to the bad job others make of it.

Although one Friend objected that "one could not take an oath of allegiance to modern governments because of the evil involved in these governments", the conclusion reached by the Conference was that "the individual must decide for himself, how far he can go in meeting the demands of the state" and that "compromise is obviously necessary if we are to live in the world at all".[32]

Austrian Quakers could not turn to a foreign Embassy to get them out of danger, as the foreign workers could. Nor could they rely on their good name to protect them, as Quakerism did not have the same connotations in Austria as it did in Germany, where the *Quäkerspeisung*, the food which American Quakers had distributed there after the first world war as part of Herbert Hoover's scheme, was still remembered with gratitude, even by some of the Nazis. In Austria, because the name "Quaker" was not used by the relief workers, people did not, on the whole, connect Quakers with the food and clothing they received during the famine. Where Quaker help was recognised, it was in connection with the support given to the Socialists in 1934, whereas the scheme to help the Nazi families in the same year had never been implemented. If it had been, it might initially have given the Quakers in Austria some sort of immunity, although it is doubtful whether it would have made any difference in the long term. Under the Nazis, where struggle and conflict were seen as necessary for strengthening the courage and resolve of the superior German race, appeals for compassion and reminders of past weakness were generally regarded with contempt and were not likely to influence the Party officials in the Quakers' favour. "Non-violence, friendship and service", the virtues extolled by German Quakers, were so opposed to the Nazi "virtues" of allegiance to the Fatherland, enmity towards any race or nation which curbed its expansion, and service seen only as unquestioning obedience to Hitler and his ruling elite that it is a wonder that the Quakers were allowed to go on with their activities at all. The Executive Committee of the German Yearly Meeting expected that the Society of Friends would eventually be suppressed and made plans for its survival as an underground organisation.[14] Thus, Hans Albrecht advised extreme caution and, unlike British and American Friends, he would obviously have preferred the Vienna Centre to emulate the Berlin Centre and distance itself from the relief work.

Although they were not directly involved in the relief work, the Viennese Friends had difficulties of their own. After Hitler's invasion of Czechoslovakia in March 1939, Jo and Biene Schindler soon had an extra complication to deal with. One of Jo Schindler's assistants in the hairdressing shop, Antonia Bruha, who had been a member of the Forum Club, worked for the Czech resistance. She was away for days at a time, helping to organise a group which carried out various acts of sabotage, such as blowing up railway lines. She knew that it would be against Jo Schindler's principles to join in such acts which endangered lives, but she was grateful to him that he never reported her frequent absences nor reproached her for them.[33] Eventually, she was picked up by the Gestapo, who threatened to harm her new-born baby if she did not give them the names of those who had helped her. When she refused, she was sent to a concentration camp, without knowing what had happened to her daughter. In fact, the child had been handed back to her husband. Antonia Bruha survived the concentration camp, and after the war she revived her friendship with Jo Schindler and his wife. She later recounted how Jo Schindler had helped many people of Czech origin when he worked as a translator for the German army of occupation in Czechoslovakia. He used his language skills to mislead the Nazis, giving answers favourable to the Czech prisoners, while pretending to translate what they had said. Under the circumstances, his interpretation of Quaker truth undoubtedly saved several lives.[34]

On 22nd August 1939, the British workers in the Centre were advised by the British Embassy to go on holiday to Switzerland, and they did not return. With the outbreak of war, the Centre was left in the capable hands of Käthe Neumayer, helped by Franz Lipovsky, who had first come into contact with the Centre when he distributed relief for the Friends after the disturbances of 1934 and who later worked for them as one of the organisers of the work camp in Marienthal. Neither he nor Käthe

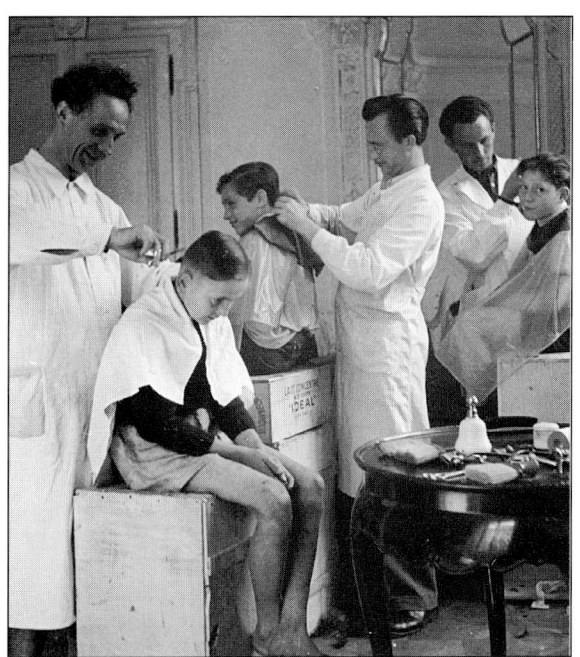

Jo Schindler, the gentle Viennese Friend, with his assistants, at the children's home he helped to found for child victims of the second world war.
(SHEILA SPIELHOFER)

Neumayer was a Quaker, but they began each day with a few minutes of Quaker silence, before they turned to the first of the desperate people waiting for their help. With the closure of the escape route to Britain, their plight was worse than ever.

NOTES
[1] Mary Campbell to Alice Nike 19th July, 1938, Letters from Vienna FSC/GE, A4. FHL.
[2] Copy of report by Bernard Lawson on a visit to Vienna for the Friends Service Council: January 21st - 26th 1939 in the possession of the writer.
[3] Mary Campbell to Alice Nike 19th July, 1938.
[4] Baroness Friederika Appel was always referred to at the Centre by this nickname.
[5] ibid.
[6] ibid.
[7] ibid.

[8] Riki Teller to Alice Nike, 29th May 1938: Letters from Vienna FSC/GE, A4, FHL.
[9] Otti Baldwin to Emma Cadbury, 15th June 1938: Letters to Vienna FSC/GE, A6. FHL. Bettelheim was detained first of all in Dachau and then in Buchenwald, before being released in April 1939. He left for the U.S.A. two weeks later.
[10] Emma Cadbury to Clarence Pickett, 12th July 1938: Letters from Vienna FSC/GE A4. FHL.
[11] Pickett 1953:146.
[12] Amery 1986: 98.
[13] Report by Bernard Lawson on a visit to Vienna for the Friends Service Council: January 21st - 26th 1939.
[14] Botz 1988: 58.
[15] Im ewigen Kampfe ist die Menschheit groß geworden - im ewigen Frieden geht sie zugrunde. (In eternal warfare mankind has become great; in eternal peace mankind would be ruined) *Mein Kampf* p 149.
[16] Interview with Alois Jalkotzy's daughter Susanne 1999.
[17] Sereny 1995: 180
[18] ibid.
[19] Speiser 1979:91.
[20] Even today, it is required of anyone who works for the State and of all students on graduation.
[21] See: *Frankfurter Zeitung* and *Neue Freie Presse*: April-August 1938, especially 1st August 1938, p.10.
[22] Factual Notes on German trip by Robert Yarnell. FSC/GE 5 FHL.
[23] "Ich werde Wien in jene Fassung bringen, die dieser Perle würdig ist" quoted in Botz 1988: 263
[24] Kenworthy 1982: 64.
[25] ibid: 264.
[26] Confidential report from Florence M. Barrow, 19th May 1938. HCSC.
[27] Ritter 1969: 29.
[28] Report of a visit to Vienna for the Friends Service Council: January 21st - 26th 1939 (in the possession of the writer).
[29] Ibid.
[30] Confidential Report on the Situation in the Vienna Group of the Society of Friends: March 1939.FSC/GE/5.
[31] Ibid.
[32] See Otto 1972 and Bailey 1994.
[33] Pickett 1953: 129-130.
[34] Tessa Cadbury to the writer 1997.
[35] Pickett 1953: 130.
[36] Pickett 1953:146.
[37] Factual Notes on German Trip by R. Yarnell, FSC/GE 5. FHL.

[38] Schmitt 1998: 137.
[39] Mary Campbell reported a conversation with Rudi Böck which reflects his conviction that Friends should "realize that England and France are to blame that the *Anschluss* did not take place immediately after the war, or later in 1931. Austria would have been saved much suffering if they had not refused to let her unite with Germany. There is no doubt that even now there will be advantages for the Austrians, greatest among them being the possibility of work. Already a number of unemployed have got jobs and they hope for large road construction schemes etc" Mary Campbell to Alice Nike 23rd March 1938. FSC/A4 FHL.
[40] For further discussion of this theory see Leon Festinger *A Theory of Cognitive Dissonance* (1957) and Jonathan Glover *The Philosophy and Psychology of Personal Identity* (1998):
"Self-deception is an easier way of maintaining present beliefs than of adopting new ones. This is because the way to retain desired beliefs is to notice and emphasise supporting evidence and to overlook or discount conflicting evidence. We cannot switch on beliefs at will".
[41] Mary Hoxie Jones writes that one of the most difficult problems faced by the group during the Schussnigg era was that of compulsory military service. She says that one of them was sentenced to three months' imprisonment with hard labour, but it has not been possible to ascertain who this was. Hoxie Jones 1937:151.
[42] Bock 1999:74.
[43] Jones 1934: 241-242.
[44] Interview with Grete Scherer 1998.
[45] Report on the Friends' World Conference: *The individual Christian and the State pp* 76-77. Woodbrooke Library.
[46] See Notes on an Arbeitsschußsitzung 31st March- 1st April 1934. FSC/GE5. FHL.
[47] Interview with Antonia Bruha 1997.
[48] ibid.

CHAPTER 12

Darkness Falls

WHEN MARGARET JONES, an American Quaker, went to Vienna from Geneva as Emma Cadbury's replacement in February 1940, Germany was already at war with England and the likelihood that America would soon join in was already in the air, so that any foreigners, especially Americans, were regarded with suspicion.

Margaret Jones soon realised that there was no longer any contact between the Vienna Group and the Centre. However, Rudi Böck did invite her to supper after she had been there for six weeks, and she looked up the Schindlers herself. She probably did not realise the danger she was putting them in, as she also did not understand Alois Jalkotzy's caution when he invited her to tea at his home and insisted on coming to the office to escort her there, as he did not want her to have to inquire the way to his flat from any of his neighbours. He could not afford to let it be known that he was entertaining foreigners.[1]

Margaret Jones was impressed by the way in which the two Austrians, Käthe Neumayer and Franz Lipovsky, had been carrying on the work:

> Bless them, how they have carried on in our name. - My hat is off to Kate Neumayer. She has done a superb piece of work. I don't think you can really visualise all that it has meant - up to a certain point, of course, because all of you have imagination, but one would have to go along with her, day by day, to really get a complete picture...Underneath is a warm heart, and outwardly there is an intense desire to have things done in a businesslike and systematic way. A keen sense of humour is quickly apparent, and I rather guess a good appraisal of character...She and Franz Lipovsky have had a little "meeting" each morning - just the two of them - perfectly valid reasons for the others not joining in the five minutes silence. At her suggestion, we have started it for all - making it very certain that no-one need attend who doesn't wish to.[2]

The staff had been cut down, so that there was only one more employee, the doorkeeper and odd-job man Schillinger, on the regular pay-roll. The "others" mentioned in this letter were temporary workers, who had lost their employment because they were "non-Aryan" and who were glad to be able to earn a little by doing clerical work at the Centre. As well as running the office and doing relief work, Käthe Neumayer had also taken over the bookkeeping. There was considerable harassment from the tax authorities, who tried to impose crippling taxes on the Centre. Refusing to give in to the demands, Käthe Neumayer reminded the tax officer that the State was benefiting from the work of the Centre:

> I told him the approximate amount which we are paying out for charity, which he found was quite a considerable sum, but he could not find any passus in the law where he could place us. I told him that for an exceptional work such as the emigration work is, he would also have to find a way to make exceptions. I explained to him that if we had to pay too heavy taxes on account of our dollar exchange, the emigration work might suffer, since I did not think the endeavours to collect dollars would continue in the same way. He said that threatening him would be of no use and I explained to him that I did not mean to threaten but to point out the consequences.[3]

She told the authorities that the Centre was now solely under the control of the AFSC in Philadelphia, and its purpose was to support the *konfessionslosen* Jews, who did not belong either to the Jewish *Kultusgemeinde* or to one of the other recognised churches, and to enable them to leave Vienna, as the Nazis wanted.[4] Käthe Neumayer's fearlessness seems to have won this particular exchange, but the restrictions on the relief work were making it increasingly difficult to carry on. All correspondence was checked, and it became very hard to find countries which would accept any more of the people desperate to get out of Germany.

Margaret Jones journeyed to Geneva and Rome, trying to convince the American authorities of the urgency of the situation, and she wrote to her friends in the USA, begging them to try to influence the government to increase the number of immigrants they would allow into the country:

> Perhaps I feel too strongly about this - but I know only too well what the life of the Jew in Vienna is today. I know of the terror and despair, and of the unbelievable difficulties each man and woman endures, and tries to solve, in connection with obtaining the US visa. I want to say again that the Vienna Consulate has on its Visa division staff men of ability and sympathy, who work as much as possible with the <u>individual</u> in mind, but they can only

do what the US immigration law permits...but it seems to me that if the US wants to make a new ruling due to the war, etc., that it must make it openly and give the reasons. We cannot continue to let these tragic people go on hoping that if they comply with every requirement, if they get all the special documents required (Marks are increasingly needed by the Jews just to <u>live</u>), if they nerve themselves for the final interview at the consulate, they <u>may</u> just possibly be the lucky ones to get visas, when we know that practically no-one is granted visas in Germany today. As thee know, the whole question of affidavits involved - irrevocable trust funds as required by the Consulate ... we cannot go out to individuals in this country for this basic co-operation when we know that regardless of what we do, he is not going to get the visa.[5]

All through the week, people were coming into the office, asking for affidavits, and the increasing poverty of the applicants meant that the Centre also had to find money for ship-passages. In February 1940, Margaret Jones reported to Philadelphia that they had already helped 60 people with money for their passage, but they had far more applicants on their lists. Since the previous October, they had received 405 applications from families and individuals, and were anxiously waiting for funds to arrive from Philadelphia.[6]

In June, the German Friend asked for by the Viennese Group arrived at last. She was Grete Sumpf, a teacher who had lost her job in 1935 through refusing to take the oath of loyalty to the State. Margaret Jones' first reaction to her was that she was not the right person for the task:

> There is such a difference between the Austrians and the Germans. The latter are so heavy and inflexible - the former just naturally gay and <u>lifted</u>. Grete is pretty good - but also school teacherish and a bit heavy. She is taking her job so seriously - and meeting with such difficulties so far as the group here is concerned.[7]

The Viennese Friends maintained that they had so many other troubles and so much to do that they had no time to meet her. Rudi Böck and his wife had joined the Red Cross, which took up most of their evenings, and the Schindlers were "so overworked they can't think". Alois Jalkotzy, who had also lost his job as a teacher, wanted to run things himself and did not take kindly to the little German schoolteacher, who "soon experienced herself how the Austrians treat the Germans - she soon realised what a terrific rift there is between the two groups".[8] All enthusiasm for the "strong German leadership" which Bernard Lawson had envisaged for the Vienna Group[9] had quite disappeared.

By July, Grete Sumpf was writing to the AFSC to tell them that she "had hardly any hope that a Quaker life can be developed with the help of our Viennese members or with that of the office for the time being".[10] Nevertheless, she tried to take a positive attitude towards Vienna and her own situation there:

> It seems to me that Vienna is the very heart of what we call "alte Deutsche geistige Kultur", grounded upon the finest spiritual heritage of the variety of nations for which the old Kaiserreich formed a political framework. For any future Middle European political unit, Austria can offer an indispensable contribution - namely, to show to what degree a nation can develop and enrich her life by allowing each of her component parts the free development of its own life and character.
>
> That heritage is hardly known among Germans. For the moment, there is a real need of better understanding between Germans and Austrians. This applies also to the Vienna Friends and to the staff of the Centre.
>
> This is the Quaker task as I see it - to live there and love and learn. It is hard to say whether anything may emerge from such an attempt that would justify the financial assistance of the American Friends Service Committee. At all events, for a long time to come there may be very, very little that can be looked upon as tangible results.[11]

In view of the political situation, the task of improving relations between Austrians and Germans that Grete Sumpf had set herself seemed doomed from the outset. The German rulers in Vienna were becoming increasingly unpopular, and disappointment and dissatisfaction with the new regime among large sections of the population made itself felt from the autumn of 1938 onwards.[12]

As Grete Sumpf did not intend to get involved in the relief work, it was not clear at first what other tasks she could be given. When Margaret Jones asked her to go to a prison with her to talk to a woman there, one of the people the Friends were hoping to help with her emigration, Grete Sumpf refused:

> Up until now, Grete has done nothing but explore possibilities for Quaker work. She has done nothing with the relief programme at the Center...Said she did not want to get mixed up yet with any of that work. I was a bit confused, because I had only wanted her to do it because she could speak German.

Käthe Neumayer did not greet the new arrival with enthusiasm either. She sent a frantic letter to the AFSC in Philadelphia, requesting confirmation of her status as acting head of the Centre whenever Margaret Jones was absent, as she felt that Grete Sumpf might have been sent to Vienna to take over the running of the Centre and that this would put an end to her relief work.[13] She still regarded the AFSC as her employers, and, indeed, they were still providing all the funding for the Centre, including Grete Sumpf"s salary.[14]

There were still an estimated 15,000 so-called "non-Aryans" in Vienna, as well as about 50,000 Jews looked after by the *Kultusgemeinde*.[15] The situation was becoming increasingly desperate for all of them, as almost all the escape routes were now closed. As they were not issued with clothing cards and their food rations were restricted, they depended on charity for survival. The *Kultusgemeinde* organised 15 soup kitchens for their members, feeding as many as 36,000 people at one point,[16] and the Quakers used part of their tight budget to provide milk for the starving people in their care, some of whom were children whose parents were in prison or who had died there. They also gave regular relief to a small number of those whose need was greatest.[17]

Käthe Neumayer, however, refused to see the situation as hopeless and continued to look for loopholes, one of her ideas being to explore the possibility of people emigrating to the USA or South America through Siberia and Japan, although both she and Margaret Jones warned their charges of the risks that this would involve. A few hundred escaped in this way.[18] As the Gildermeester organisation had been closed by the government at the beginning of 1940, the Quakers were now the only ones to whom the non-religious Jews could turn.

The American Quakers had to face the possibility that their work in Europe might be coming to an end, and so they began to make provisions for what would happen after they left. Once more, there were considerable differences between the attitudes in Berlin and Vienna. In Berlin, the Quakers were troubled by the growing animosity towards anyone who helped the Jews. They were afraid that they might soon share the fate of many of those from other churches who had been imprisoned and sent to the concentration camps. When Howard Elkington, the American representative from the Berlin Centre, who was suffering from severe depression as a result of the strain caused by his work, went to Vienna to consult with her, Margaret Jones found that their views about the future differed and that "Berlin does NOT understand Vienna". [19]She was annoyed that Elkington assumed that both the centres would close if no more Americans could be found to work there, whereas Margaret Jones insisted that if she left, Käthe Neumayer and Franz Lipovsky would "just naturally carry on". Both she and Elkington returned to the States in the summer of 1940.

After returning to Philadelphia, Margaret Jones was able to write freely about her experiences in Vienna, especially about the sufferings of the Jews:

> Then suddenly the Italian border closed - and life a bleak empty nothingness, with increasing physical suffering. For Jews have no clothing cards - can buy no clothing; Jews have to buy their food after the Aryans have bought their rations from the severely restricted supplies; Jews are being herded into the ghetto, not yet as drastically as Warsaw, but increasingly bad; Jews are forbidden entrance to the Opera, movies, parks, cafes - My dears, I frankly admit to all that I could stand that only six months. I had to leave - the end of August - and of course, now I long to be back in Vienna again! Such darling friends I have there, Jews and Gentiles - brave and hopeful, and trying not to hate...[20]

She tried to give Käthe Neumayer her support and ensure that the relief work went on. In reply to desperate requests from the Vienna Centre, Mary Hoxie Jones, Margaret's friend and ally at the AFSC office, assured Käthe Neumayer that her authority was unquestioned and that Grete Sumpf had been sent to the Centre only to support Viennese Quakers and not to take charge of the Centre:

> Everyone has felt that she would be an excellent person for this service and as far as I have been able to tell, German meeting has been interested in doing what it could to help bring Vienna Friends in contact with one another... Therefore, we have encouraged Grete to do what she can. Frankly, it never occurred to me that she would be put in charge of the Centre. I have heard nothing from either Mr Elkington or Margaret of such a move and I read your letter with real dismay. It may be, of course, that such a step was taken in view of the necessity, forced by present conditions, to have a person of Grete Sumpf's nationality in charge - a technical arrangement which you and she can work out together...It would seem in the light of the possibility of starting transportation via Siberia and also of doing relief that we still have a real service to render at Singerstrasse...[21]

However, other AFSC workers felt that responsibility for the Vienna Centre should be transferred to the German Yearly Meeting. They were afraid that the Nazi authorities were looking for a pretext to proceed against the Centres in Berlin or Vienna and probably thought that Käthe Neumayer, with her outspoken fearlessness in dealing with the Nazis, might endanger them all.

Douglas Steere,[22] a representative of AFSC, who shared Hans Albrecht's view that both the Berlin and the Vienna Centre should concentrate on Quaker spirituality rather than on relief work, visited the

Vienna Centre in the autumn of 1940 and afterwards sent a telegram from Germany to the Philadelphia central office, asking the AFSC to confirm the authority of the German Executive Committee to take decisions regarding the Vienna office:

> AFTER THOROUGH INSPECTION VIENNA QUAKER BUREAU NEW YEARLY MEETING COMMITTEE REACHED FORMULA KEEPING SUMPF NEUMAYER LIPOVSKY SCHILLINGER. ONE TYPIST. DISMISSION OTHERS JANUARY FIRST. MAKING JOINT WORK SUMPF NEUMAYER WITH COORDINATION VIENNA BY KENWORTHY. VISIT EACH TWO MONTHS. HOPE PHILADELPHIA RESPECTS NEW AUTHORITY GIVEN COMMITTEE HERE.[23]

In the Berlin Centre it was decided to put into operation what was called the "stormy weather plan". In March 1941, the Committee decided that all instructions covering possible relief activities must thenceforth be signed by the clerk of the GYM, adding: "L. S. Kenworthy's name should not appear, as the American Friends no longer direct the Berlin Centre". The same committee also reminded everyone that Friends were "a Religious Society and ... the religious side of the work should appear in any statement of an official nature". Howard Elkington, who returned once more to Europe on a visit in June 1941, reported that the "German Committee can really function without us".[24] Soon afterwards, Kenworthy, the last American representative, left Germany.

Despite Käthe Neumayer's misgivings, the future of the Vienna Centre, too, now rested with Hans Albrecht.

NOTES

[1] Margaret Jones to Mary Hoxie Jones: 6th July 1940: AFSC.
[2] Margaret Jones to the Refugee Office in Philadelphia: 25th February 1940: AFSC.
[3] Käthe Neumayer to Mary Rogers: 9th April 1940: AFSC.
[4] According to Martin Gilbert, nearly half the Jews of Austria, more than ninety-eight thousand, left for other lands (Gilbert: 63). This figure probably does not include those who were Jewish only according to Nazi concepts and who were referred to as "Christian non-Aryans" in Nazi terminology. More than 24,000 persons who had renounced Judaism but had Jewish grandparents were classified as Jews. See *Demographie of Austrian Jews 1938-1945* in *Judenplatz: Place of Remembrance*. Wien 2000; Pichler Verlag.
[5] Margaret Jones to Clarence Pickett: n.d.: AFSC.
[6] Margaret Jones to Mary Hoxie Jones: 28th March 1940: AFSC.
[7] Margaret Jones to Mary Hoxie Jones: 6th July 1940: AFSC.
[8] ibid.

9 See above: 63.
10 Grete Sumpf to Friends in Philadelphia: 19th July 1940: AFSC.
11 Ibid.
12 For a description of the growing discontent and opposition to the new regime, especially after the beginning of 1939, when a number of unpopular laws were introduced, see Botz 1988: 465ff.
13 There seems little doubt that Käthe Neumayer had been given the assurance that she should act as head of the Centreas an official Handbook of the Society of Friends published in Philadelphia in October 1941 notes " An Austrian woman long associated with the Centre was made acting director in the absence of English and American friends". Woodbrooke Library.
14 Käthe Neumayer to Emma Cadbury: 27th November 1940: AFSC.
15 Report from Margaret Jones in Geneva: July 8th 1940: AFSC.
16 Margaret Jones to Friends in Geneva and Philadelphia: 3 May 1940: AFSC.
17 A Budget per Month submitted by Margaret Jones for 1940 gives the amount used for relief as 5000 German Marks, with 500 of this for milk, from a total expenditure of 7370 German Marks. This did not include passage money.
18 Report from Margaret Jones in Philadelphia: January 1941.: AFSC.
19 Margaret Jones to Mary Hoxie Jones: 6th July 1940: AFSC.
20 Margaret Jones to Clarence Pickett November 1940: AFSC.
21 Mary Oaxie Jones to Käthe Neumayer. 25th July 1940; AFSC.
22 11 American Friends travelled as Commissioners to all the European Centres, using Berlin as their headquarters. Handbook of the Religious Society of Friend: Philadelphia October 1941.
23 Steere to AFSC 8th November 1940: AFSC.
24 For these details about the developments in Berlin, I am indebted to the article by J. Roger Carter The Quaker International Centre in Berlin 1920-1942 in *The Journal of the Friends' Historical Society* Vol.6 1990 and to the research of Professor Hans Schmitt, published in his book *Quakers & Nazis: Inner Light in Outer Darkness (*see *Bibliography).* At the latter's suggestion, I have tried to fill in one of the gaps in his account by chronicling the story from the Vienna end.

CHAPTER 13

Closing the Doors

WHEN THE FIRST large deportations of Austrian Jews to Poland was carried out in October 1940, Heydrich, the head of the *Sicherheitspolizei* (the dreaded Nazi special police) had their neighbours in Vienna watched in order to see what the reaction would be. His agents reported that no-one seemed to have taken much notice.[1]

Many people have asked themselves how it was possible for people to ignore such happenings. The psychologist Daniel Goleman discusses this phenomenon and comes to the conclusion that anything which causes intense anxiety or pain may be kept from our conscious view and so out of what he calls our "frame".[2] This primitive response to danger is a narrowing of the vision which allows us to protect ourselves and our families when our survival is threatened. Two years of Nazi rule and the added uncertainty of wartime had obviously had this effect on most of the Viennese. In spite of this lack of protest, the deportations did stop for a time. Whether the reason for this was because the Nazis feared adverse reactions or whether it was because they needed the trains for the war effort cannot now be ascertained.

One person who had noticed what was happening was Käthe Neumeyer, who redoubled her efforts to get those who were threatened out of Vienna. By the end of 1939, however, only a few people were still able to find a way of escape because most countries, including the USA, had practically closed their doors to Jews.[3] Some still managed to make their way southwards through Yugoslavia, Romania and Turkey, hoping to be able to go on to Palestine. A few did manage to enter the United States and Latin America, others went to Shanghai.[4] The Nazis explained that the Jews were being resettled in the General Government, as German-occupied Poland was called, to work for the German war effort. As conditions in Vienna were becoming increasingly difficult, many of the deportees were initially quite willing to go, as they reasoned that as long as their work was of value to Germany, they would not be in such great danger.

When the deportations started again in the February of the following year, Käthe Neumayer once more risked her own safety, this time by telephoning to Leonard Kenworthy in Berlin, asking him to come immediately to Vienna, as she thought that he would be able to confirm that several of the people who had been ordered to prepare for deportation would soon be in receipt of papers allowing them to emigrate. She obviously also hoped to make use of the fact that the regime was still anxious not to draw too much attention to its persecution of the Jews and was nervous of its reputation in the U.S.A. Kenworthy took the next train to Vienna and from there he telephoned to someone in the United States consulate in Philadelphia who was able to send a list of those whose emigration papers were in preparation there. With these details, Käthe Neumayer was able to obtain the release of a few people. Unfortunately, the Nazis then filled up the number of those to be deported by ordering other Jews to take their place. Kenworthy stayed for a few days in the Vienna Centre and experienced how depressing it was to have to admit that there was not much more he could do for the masses of desperate people who streamed into the Centre every day. He said they were the worst days of his whole life.[5]

On her return from a holiday in February 1941, Grete Sumpf wrote to a friend, Cilli Seutemann,[6] a Jewish Quaker who lived near the Quaker house in Bad Pyrmont in Germany, telling her that she had heard that 1000 people had been told that they had two days in which to get ready for the next transport. They were to be allowed to take 50kg of luggage with them, as well as some money, although they were not told how much. Grete Sumpf also heard that it was planned to send a number of similar trainloads over the next few weeks, 60,000 people altogether. Only those who could prove that they were likely to get emigration papers in the near future were able to get their departure postponed.[7]

A few days later, she wrote again, saying that the first transport had already left, with 1000 people from every age group on board, men, women and children. They had first been collected together in two schools, where all their money had been taken from them, and each person had then been given the small sum of 40 Zloty, regardless of how much they had handed over. They also had to sign a declaration that they were going of their own free will and that they had bequeathed their possessions to the State. Only a few had been able to take a sack filled with straw with them to sleep on. A second transport was already being prepared for departure on the following Wednesday.[8]

Käthe Neumayer and Grete Sumpf seem to have forgotten their differences in their desire to help the poor people who had to prepare for this journey into the unknown. While Käthe Neumayer went on with her efforts to find ways of escape, Grete Sumpf concentrated on those for whom escape now seemed impossible. One of the great problems was that many of the Viennese Jews were by this time so desperately poor that they had nothing to take with them on their journey to Poland, no money, no suitcase, and no decent clothing, as they had already had to pawn anything of value in order to stay alive. The most difficult thing was to find shoes, especially for the children.

Grete Sumpf again wrote to Cilli Seutemann, asking her to beg the German Friends for help. Some of the women immediately came to her assistance, and soon packets and suitcases full of warm clothing, as well as money, started arriving every day in the Centre. A sewing circle, composed of people who were themselves threatened with deportation, sorted and mended the clothes and arranged them in piles in a special room so that people could quickly and easily find what they needed. But the clothes were only sufficient to meet the needs of about a tenth of those who came to the Centre, begging for help. Grete Sumpf had to write again, saying that they had already received 36 packages but desperately needed still more, although she knew how difficult it was for her friends to send them:

> If you could draw the attention of other acquaintances to our plight, we should be very grateful. There are all kinds of things stored up in the households of old people that would be valuable to us, things that they don't use very often, for example, we cut up old moth-eaten things to wrap round people's feet as shoes, from old potato sacks we sew rucksacks or we use them to pack bedding in. We use bits of braid or carpeting to fasten up the rucksacks. Any rags that are of no use for anything else are used as filling for quilts, which we sew from any old pieces of cloth, such as old curtains...We have given away all the toys and children's books and would be especially grateful for any replacements.[9]

She reminded her friends that such things might mean the difference between life and death to those on the transport. From what the relief workers had heard from the people who had survived the journey the year before, it made all the difference to their chances of survival if people were able to set out in a relatively optimistic frame of mind. Some of them even welcomed the idea of being sent somewhere where they thought they might be able to find work, as they felt that conditions in Vienna were insupportable. Others wondered why so many old people and children were being deported, if the aim was to make use of their working capacities.

The workers at the Centre prepared a list of the most necessary things which the outcasts should take with them, and gave a lot of practical advice, which they hoped would ensure that nothing was lost or stolen on the journey. Having realised that there was no point in anyone trying to take money with them, they used the money sent by the German Friends to buy simple medicines, such as aspirin and charcoal tablets. One of the German Friends deliberately fastened cheap jewellery onto the old clothes she sent, as she thought that the deportees would be able to use it to barter for eggs and butter once they reached Poland.[10]

Some of the German friends wrote that it would be better to help only a few rather than spreading the help too thinly.[11] However, the misery of all those who asked for help was so great that they could not be refused. The Centre no longer made any distinction between the religious Jews and the "non-Aryan Christians" or those of no religion, but helped all those who turned to them as well as they could.

It was not only material help that they wanted. Grete Sumpf wrote:

> Some people come to me and say, "I don't want anything from you, I just want to talk to you". One highly intelligent woman said, "If we have to go to Poland, we have to see it as a very important task. But I don't know yet how to tackle it". A musician said, "If I could take a musical instrument with me, I would be able to console many people with my music". So she decided to learn the recorder. She did not mention that she is severely handicapped and has no boots. Three people came to tell me about their worries about the illegitimate children of mixed blood (*Mischlingskinder*) that they were having to leave behind. Another left her old mother in my care.[12]

Grete Sumpf felt that it was especially important to keep up the spirits of those still waiting for deportation, as far as that was humanly possible:

> The experiences of last year as well as those of this year show that the state of mind of those preparing for deportation makes a decisive difference. The reports we receive from Poland are practically unanimous in stressing that while some people are completely broken by the experience and overwhelmed by shame and misery, others show a remarkable courage. And those who can accept their dreadful fate as a task laid on them by God seem to be unshakeable. We experience real greatness among those in our care, especially among the voluntary helpers and temporary workers, who only occasionally refer in a brief remark to the fact that they, too, are among those who are in danger.[13]

One worry which some of them expressed was that those who did not belong to the Jewish faith might be boycotted in Poland by the religious Jews, so that they wondered whether they should keep quiet about it, but Grete Sumpf discussed the problem with them and they came to the conclusion that it would soon be discovered and would show that they had no real religious conviction, as true religion cannot be hidden. On the other hand, the witness of genuine Christianity will not awaken any resentment on the part of pious Jews but rather their respect, as many experiences have shown.[14]

On 24th February, Grete Sumpf wrote that she had read some cards that had arrived from those sent on the first transport. Later, similar news was received from the second transport, which had arrived in Kielce. Several thousand deportees from Vienna were eventually crowded into the city, where there were already sixteen thousand Jews living in appalling conditions.[15]

On 17th March, Grete Sumpf wrote to her friend in Germany that, after five such transports had left, each with about a thousand people on board, the people on the sixth list were sent home from the school where they had been waiting and told that for the moment no more would be sent to Poland. Some people said they had been told, "not until September".

As David S. Wyman points out, [16] the transportation of Jews across Europe seriously hampered the German war effort by overtaxing the railways and tying down administrative and military resources. At the same time, although millions of extra workers would have been needed for the war industry, the senseless hatred of the Jews stopped the Nazis from using the skills of even those who were highly qualified. They were condemned to hunger and misery, whether they remained in Vienna or were hoarded into the already overcrowded ghettos in Poland.

Obviously, the responsibilities of the three workers in the Centre, Käthe Neumayer, Grete Sumpf and Franz Lipovsky, were becoming almost more than they could cope with. They were able to report that not too many of the people who had been giving them voluntary help had been deported, but they were all in a state of unbearable tension. Some who had been rescued from deportation now had nowhere to live, as their houses had been confiscated by the Nazis. Grete Sumpf wrote asking for permission to use some of the money which German Friends had contributed to pay for lodgings for them. She thought it was necessary to carry on with the circle of voluntary helpers, even though only two of the helpers were able to come regularly. The others came sporadically, as they had so many difficulties to cope with, and "we do not know how long we will be able to keep any of them".[17] One of their tasks was to prepare parcels of English books and musical instruments for prisoner-of-war camps. They also went on with the sewing circle, trying to make serviceable clothing out of the old garments they had received.

In addition to all their other work, the Centre workers took on the task of finding sympathetic doctors and chemists who were still willing to help and of going to purchase necessary goods in those shops where it would have been dangerous for Jews to attempt it. Grete Sumpf organised Bible study circles for those who showed interest, as well as musical evenings, to distract people from the increasing difficulties and uncertainties of their everyday lives.

Another great worry was how to keep in touch with those who had been deported. The Centre received requests from Poland for clothing and shoes. When they tried to send parcels from Vienna, the post office refused to accept them, so that Grete Sumpf had to appeal once more to her friends in Germany. She could not bear the idea that those who had trusted her might think she had forgotten them. She sent addresses and parcels to Germany, asking her friends to forward the goods to Poland, but it was difficult to arrange at a distance, especially as not all of her letters arrived at their destination and there was always the fear of endangering her friends or of putting too much of a burden on them.[18]

When she travelled to Berlin on 28th February to report to the Executive Committee of the German Yearly Meeting about the situation in Vienna, Grete Sumpf seems to have been warned that she must not endanger the existence of Quakerism as a whole by drawing too much attention to herself or to Cilli Seutermann, as she writes to her friend on 24th May 1941:

> In Berlin we had extensive discussions about sending parcels. Margarete has no difficulties with it and therefore she asked me to send her a parcel. I suggested to Mizi that I should do the same with her, i.e. send her material, but I do not yet know if she has the time to make all the further arrangements. I am not allowed to do that from here. I think you have less freedom than the others, because you, too, represent "Quakerism" in some sense. The others also all thought that we had to take that into consideration. I have often felt bitterly, here and also in Berlin, how much of one's freedom of action one sacrifices when one is no longer completely a private person but a representative of a group or organisation. But that can't be altered now. Margarete said that she could not take on any new people, although she has no reservations about going on caring for the old ones. I am, of course, particularly concerned about some of my former protégés, who relied on my loyalty and who are certainly already disappointed. So I can only leave it to you, whether I should send a parcel to you, too, and give you the names of a few people…One thing is certain, after the experiences in Berlin and other places, we must be

very cautious about anything which might be connected with the German Yearly Meeting...[19]

Cilli Seutemann must have been in a particularly precarious situation but she went on sending parcels to the addresses sent to her from Vienna. One of these addresses was that of a young woman called Steffi Telheim, who had been deported on the first transport on 15th February to Opole, near Lublin. She wrote to her mother, whom she had left in Grete Sumpf's care, saying that she had been taken in by good people and had a bed to sleep in, unlike some of the others who had been quartered in a Jewish temple and in schools. She had also managed to keep her belongings, but she asked Grete to send her bedding and money.[20] Later she wrote that she had succeeded in getting a job in the post office and was even earning money. Grete praised her as a sensible and practical woman, who was using her position not only for her own advantage but also for the good of the whole group.[21]

Perhaps the help and encouragement she had received from the Quakers did strengthen Steffi Telheim's determination to survive. In October 1941, she managed to flee from the ghetto and return to Vienna. One can only imagine what dangers she must have endured during the journey and how many people must have risked their lives to help her. She and her sister Adele, who had been told to report for deportation, were taken in and hidden by acquaintances, who lived on the fourth floor of a house in the centre of Vienna and who misled the Gestapo by reporting that the two sisters had fled to Budapest. In spite of searches by the police and frequent bombing raids, in which the terrified women could not seek shelter in the cellars, as there were Nazis living in the same house, they managed to escape discovery. Tragically, Steffi fell ill as the result of an illness that she had contracted in Poland. By July 1944, her condition was so bad that her friends tried to get her into a hospital under a false name, knowing that they were putting all their lives at risk. When this failed, they called in two doctors who promised to keep their secret and who kept their word. In spite of their efforts, the patient's condition worsened still further, and mental problems aggravated the situation both for her and for those who were trying to save her life.

On 23rd October 1944, three years after her return to Vienna, Steffi Telheim died, leaving her friends faced with the almost insoluble problem of disposing of her body. After several unsuccessful attempts at smuggling the body out of the house, they began to contemplate suicide as the only way out of an unbearable situation. At the last moment, two members of the resistance movement turned up and constructed a metal coffin in which they transported the body to the cellar, past the doors of the unsuspecting Nazis. At the risk of their lives, they spent days digging a hole in the cellar in which to bury the improvised coffin.

Adele was still alive when Vienna was freed from the Nazis but she died three months later in July 1945, as a result of the deprivations she had suffered and especially the fearful experience of her sister's death.[22]

Another of the people on Cilli Seutermann's list, Jolante Spohrer, a generous, energetic woman of over seventy, wrote to Grete Sumpf:

> As my only pair of shoes is finished, I turn to you with confidence. Above all, I need a pair of snowshoes, size 43. We are suffering great deprivation. In God's name, do not forget us!

Immediately, Grete Sumpf packed shoes and stockings in separate packages and tried to send them to her, but the post office once again refused to accept them. Grete wrote to her friend Cilli that she was convinced that Jolante Spohrer, who had shown great courage and even humour when she was preparing for the deportation, would come to terms with even the most difficult circumstances, although she had "obviously found the conditions much more difficult than she expected".[23] Jolante Spohrer wrote from Modliborzyce in the district of Lublin, where the conditions were not quite as bad as in some of the other camps and where there was at least rudimentary medical care for the 998 men, women and children who had been sent there from Vienna, as they included 22 qualified doctors. Nevertheless, only 13 people are known to have survived this camp, and Jolante Spohrer's name is not among them.[24]

In addition to all her other worries, Grete Sumpf was also troubled that she had not succeeded in the task for which she had been sent to Vienna, that of supporting the Vienna Group:

> Joe Schindler's mother died a few days ago and I only heard about it on Saturday when I phoned. That shows how little I have been able to concern myself with them. Rudi Böck was here a short time ago on leave, and I was not able to accept their invitation to meet them all. I will only be able gradually to pick up the relationships for which I originally came here.[25]

There were added tensions because Hans Albrecht, who was still Clerk of the German Yearly Meeting,[26] wanted to dismiss the other workers at the Centre and had already given them notice. Understandably, he felt responsible for the safety of German Quakers and insisted that, like the Berlin Centre, the Vienna Centre should concentrate on spiritual matters rather than functioning as a relief organisation. He disregarded the fact that, from the very beginning, the Vienna Centre had been run on quite different lines. Those foreign Friends, such as Howard Elkington and Douglas Steere, who had worked with Albrecht in Berlin and who knew the situation in Vienna only from short visits, tended to agree with him, whereas those who had spent more time in Vienna and knew how different the situation was from that in Germany, tended to sympathise with

Käthe Neumayer's point of view. However, apart from sending her money to keep the office going, there was little they could do to support her.

Käthe Neumayer, who still insisted that she had been put in charge of the office by both the British and the American Quakers and had documents to prove it, bitterly resented Albrecht's assuming control, especially as she felt that closing the office would be a betrayal of all the persecuted people who regarded her as their last hope. Grete Sumpf must have felt trapped between loyalty to the German Yearly Meeting and the personal sympathy and wholehearted admiration she felt for Käthe Neumayer and Franz Lipovsky, which had replaced the original animosity between them and transformed her whole attitude towards the Vienna Centre. She tried to point out that no-one from outside could really judge the situation. Anyone who had witnessed what Käthe Neumayer had achieved could not fail to sympathise with her point of view.[27] However, Hans Albrecht remained adamant, at any rate as far as Käthe Neumayer was concerned. She was given a month's notice and finally dismissed at the end of September 1941. Franz Lipovsky, who was not in immediate danger of being called up because he held a Czech passport and suffered from health problems, was kept on for another year, until the Centre was finally closed in the autumn of 1942.[28]

In a letter to the AFSC in October 1941, Albrecht defends his treatment of Käthe Neumayer, saying that she had intrigued against him, and, anyway, she would not have any trouble in finding alternative employment, as "the situation on the labour market in Germany is such that anyone who wants to work can find a post and is well paid".[29] He asks the Americans only to consult the Vienna Centre in future on those refugee cases where there was a reasonable hope of a positive outcome, as "anything else only serves to awaken false hopes". He goes on to say:

> It is, therefore, our whole aim and our deepest wish to keep the office in Vienna on, if it is at all possible, in order to strengthen the spiritual and religious tasks, as that is the basis and core of all our work. And here I must add another few words. It is only natural that Emma Cadbury and all of you feel loyalty towards someone who worked there for over twenty years, and we, too, have fully taken her feelings into account. I have repeatedly told her how much I understand what it must mean to her to leave this work, which has become her life work...However, she had no understanding of what Quakerism is and aims at. She told us quite openly that she had no interest in the religious side of Quakerism and that she did not know what Grete Sumpf wanted to do in Vienna after the relief work finished. And that after twenty years of shared work!... Fräulein N. is, without doubt, a very competent worker, but she is definitely no Quaker.[30]

In fact, even if she had not been dismissed, Käthe Neumayer would not have been able to go on with her work much longer. Although she and her fellow workers were aware of the harsh conditions in the ghettos in Poland, they thought at first that the Jewish people had been sent there to work. Initially, the ghettos had been relatively "open", that is, people were able to go in and out and they were allowed to communicate to a limited extent with their friends and relatives. But after Hitler had decided on the total extermination of the Jews in July 1941, the ghettos were gradually closed, and by October 1941, any Jew trying to leave the ghetto was threatened with the death penalty. Anyone trying to help Jews to escape was similarly punished. In the same month, it was forbidden for any Jew to leave either Germany or any of the occupied territories. Thus, all hope of legal emigration was also finished.

Several psychologists have tried to analyse what it was which made people like Käthe Neumayr able to go on struggling to stem the tide of cruelty and indifference which threatened to engulf them and to persist in their efforts at helping the Jews in spite of the danger to themselves, whereas most people protect themselves in such situations by closing their conscious minds to whatever causes them intense anxiety or pain.[31] One of the necessary qualities of such "rescuers" seems to be a sense of "competency", that is, the confidence that they can alter events for the better. Many people, even Hans Albrecht, commented on this quality in Käthe Neumayer. Working for the Quakers in a position of trust and responsibility for so many years and seeing that it was possible to alleviate suffering enabled her to feel that her work mattered and that she could do it well.

After the British and American Friends left the Vienna Centre, she must have felt that she was the only one left who had the knowledge and resources to help at least some of the persecuted people to escape. Others who might have wanted to help had neither the same skills nor the same opportunities as Käthe Neumayer. The fact that she was single also gave her a certain freedom not enjoyed by those who were afraid of endangering their whole family if they exposed themselves too much. She was also able to inspire Grete Sumpf, another single woman, with similar courage. Nevertheless, her ability to persevere for years in circumstances which daunted other people after a few days defies explanation.

Grete Sumpf seems to have stayed on a few months longer. Her last letter to Cilli Seutemann before leaving Vienna, written in November 1941, shows how isolated she had become, but her compassion for the Jews, now hopelessly trapped and deprived of all human rights, was stronger than ever:

I wish I could have you here with me! The suffering here is boundless - it affects about 60,000 people![32] And I am so alone in carrying on the work which you already know so much about. Think of me sometimes![33]

The office closed down, shortly after it had moved to new premises away from the Singerstrasse, which has been the scene of so many joys and sorrows.[34]

NOTES

[1] Stolzfus 1996: 6.
[2] For a discussion of Daniel Goleman*s theories in relation to the attitudes of people towards the persecution of the Jews see: Fogelman E. *Conscience and Courage: Rescuers of Jews during the Holocaust.* New York: Anchor 1992.
[3] The USA had opened the borders a little more at the beginning of 1938 but began to close them again in the autumn of 1939. See: Wyman 1984: 12.
[4] Kenworthy 1982:33.
[5] ibid: 36.
[6] Just before the outbreak of war, Cilli Seutermann sent her small daughter to safety in England but she herself stayed with her non-Jewish husband in Bad Pyrmont. The townspeople there did not at first realize that she was Jewish. To escape deportation, she was later forced into hiding.
[7] Grete Sumpf to Cilly Seutemann, 18th February 1941: Seutemann File FHL.
(All translations of these letters by the author
[8] ibid.
[9] Grete Sumpf to Friends in Germany 7th March 1941: Seutemann File FHL.
[10] Cilli Seutemann to Grete Sumpf, 18th February 1941: Seutemann File FHL.
[11] Grete Sumpf to Friends in Germany 17th March 1941: Seutemann File FHL.
[12] Grete Sumpf to Friends in Germany 7th March 1941:Seutemann File FHL.
[13] Grete Sumpf to Friends in Germany 7th March 1941: Seutemann File FHL.
[14] Grete Sumpf to Friends in Germany 10th March 1941: Seutemann File FHL.
[15] Gilbert 1987: 146.

[16] Wyman 1984: 13.
[17] Grete Sumpf to Friends in Germany 17th March 1941: Seutemann File FHL.
[18] Grete Sumpf to Cilli Seutemann 24th May and 21st & 23rd June, 1941: Seutemann File FHL.
[19] Grete Sumpf to Cilli Seutemann 24th May 1941: Seutemann File FHL. The "Margarete" mentioned here was Margarete Lachmund, a Quaker from Berlin, had been organising the sending of parcels to the Jewish communities in Poland since the invasion of Poland at the beginning of the war. (See: Bailey 1994: 137). "Mizi" was a Jewish "friend of the Friends", Henriette Jordan. She was arrested with several other people during a Quaker Meeting in Berlin in December 1942 and spent Christmas in prison, whereas the others were released immediately. Mizi was freed three weeks later after the intervention of her "Aryan" husband. (See: *Lebensbilder deutscher Quäker während der NS-Herrschaft 1933-45:* 45. A slightly different version of this incident is given in *Bailey* 1994: 153). Like Cilli Seutermann, Mizi Jordan had to go into hiding in 1944 to avoid deportation.
[20] Grete Sumpf to Cilli Seutermann 24th February 1941: Seutemann File FHL.
[21] Undated list of addresses with comments sent to Cilli Seutermann: Seutemann File FHL.
[22] Information from the Documentation Archive of the Austrian Resistance, Vienna.
[23] Undated list of addresses with comments sent to Cilli Seutermann: Seutemann File FHL.
[24] Information from the Documentation Archive of the Austrian Resistance, Vienna.
[25] Grete Sumpf to Friends in Germany 17th March, 1941: Seutemann File FHL.
[26] Hans Albrecht was Clerk of the German Yearly Meeting for twenty years, from 1927 to 1947, an unusually long period of office, as normally the length of service for Quakers is limited to three or at most six years.
[27] Grete Sumpf to Friends in Germany 7th March 1941: Seutemann File FHL.
[28] Closing the Centre proved a more lengthy process than Hans Albrecht had anticipated, according to a testimonial given to Franz Lipovsky by Hans Albrecht in September 1942. (Original document in the possession of Frau Lipovsky).
[29] Hans Albrecht to Mary Hoxie Jones, 7th October 1941: AFSC Archives, Philadelphia.
(writer's translation from the German original).

[30] Ibid.
[31] For an analysis of the qualities of the "rescuer", see Fogelman 1992 (*Conscience and Courage*) and Midlarsky 1984 (*Competence and Helping*).
[32] From early 1941 onwards about 48,000 people were deported from Vienna to ghettos, concentration and extermination camps. Only 1,700 survived. See *Demographie of Austrian Jews 1938-1945* in *Judenplatz: Place of Remembrance*. Wien 2000; Pichler Verlag.
[33] Grete Sumpf to Cilli Seutemann, 10th November 1941: Seutemann File FHL.
[34] The furniture and office equipment were stored in a warehouse; they were later destroyed. Lawson MS: 23.

Epilogue

WHEN THE FIRST American and British Quakers arrived in Vienna after the war, in May 1946, they immediately got in touch with the remaining members of the Vienna Group, who were already holding regular meetings in the house of Jo and Bine Schindler. All of them had survived, if not untouched, with at least no acute visible signs of the horrors they had just been through.

Having refused a commission and served as a platoon builder in the German army, Rudi Böck returned to his civilian occupation as an architect for the Vienna Municipal Council, but his health had been seriously undermined.[1] His flat had been ransacked during his absence, and his wife and small daughter had fled to the Tyrol in 1945. After an adventurous flight, they returned to find that their house and all their possessions had disappeared.[2]

Alois Jalkotzy had been called up in the last weeks of the war, when young boys and old men were sent to the front in a last desperate effort to hold off defeat. One of his two sons, Hannes, who had worked as a medical orderly and interpreter in the army, returned to Vienna in 1946, after being a prisoner of war in British hands. The other son, Peter, had been killed near Leningrad in 1943.[3] In spite of his age, Alois Jalkotzy took over the administration of a remand home in Eggenburg, about eighty kilometres to the north of Vienna, where he tried to rehabilitate boys whose only crime was to put into practice the lessons for survival they had learned during six years of war.[4]

During the war, the Schindlers had taken a German Friend, Käthe Tacke, into their home so that she could escape the bombing in Berlin and wait in the comparative safety of Vienna until the child she was expecting had been born. Now they also took in some of the neglected children who were roaming the streets of Vienna, some of them with no knowledge of their own name or identity. With the help and financial support of Swedish, Danish and Swiss Friends and other welfare agencies, such as the Red Cross and Swiss Aid, a project was set up in a large house in Dornbach, a residential suburb of Vienna, where some of these children could be housed and helped to recover from their traumatic experiences. All of the Friends supported this home with whatever skills they had. Rudi Böck helped to adapt the rooms to their new purpose and, even after he had been reproached for showing no outward contrition for his support of the Nazis and his attendance at Meetings for Worship ceased, he went on giving the Vienna Group valuable support and advice and remained a Quaker till his death.[5] Jo Schindler turned up regularly to cut the childrens' hair, and Käthe Tacke lived in the house for a few weeks at the beginning, until other workers from Switzerland, Austria and Denmark took over and she could return to Germany. The boys from Alois Jalkotzy's remand home made quite a lot of the furniture. Again the Friends had found a task which served to unite them.

Both Emma Cadbury and Margaret Jones journeyed to Vienna as soon as possible, to see what had happened to their many friends there. They found Käthe Neumayer, thin and hungry, but ready to help them with setting up relief structures in a country once more threatened with starvation.[6] In September 1946, Bernard Lawson, too, returned to Vienna to renew contacts with the Austrian Friends, who, by this time, were holding Meeting for Worship fortnightly in the Children's Home. He was appalled at the damage that had been done to the beautiful city and at the dreadful poverty to which his Viennese friends were once more reduced:

> I experienced something of what life was like under the "Four Power Occupation". I was compelled to stay in a hotel occupied by the British Army and live on rations provided by them. One of the hardest things was not to be able to invite my Austrian Friends out for a meal, and they themselves were so short of food I did not like accepting their hospitality, even when offered. Sometimes I saved a bread roll or some other bit of food from my breakfast, to take to someone I was due to visit.[7]

Although there was no Centre, relief work had started once more and was being carried on from offices in various parts of the city, which was divided into four zones under the control of the Allied troops. Thanks to Rudi Böck's efforts, new premises were soon allocated to the Friends by the City Council, and a new centre was opened there in 1948, this time named simply Quaker House.[8]

NOTES

[1] Greenwood 1975: 325.
[2] Woodbrooke Journal 1948.
[3] Woodbrooke Journal 1946.
[4] Some of Alois Jalkotzy's innovative ideas for eradicating the effects of Nazi indoctrination can be seen in the *Mappe der Menschlichkeit*, a magazine produced regularly by the boys, giving descriptions of people who were truly humane and could serve them as examples.

[5] Interviews with Grete Scherer and Antonia Bruha, 1997. See also *Lebensbilder deutsche Quäker während der NS-Herrschaft 1933-1945:*112.
[6] *Vienna in the Spring* Report by Margaret E. Jones 26th April 1946. AFSC.
[7] Lawson MS: 23.
[8] Lawson MS: 24.

Bibliography

Atherton Smith A *The Austrian Land Settlements* London: The Friends Council for International Service 1926.

Bartlett C.J. *Global Conflict 1880-1970* London: Longman 1984.

Bailey B. *A Quaker Couple in Germany* York: Sessions 1994.

Bane S. L. and Lutz R.H. Organization of American Relief in Europe, 1918-1919, Stanford: Stanford University Press 1943.

Bauer O. Die österreichische Revolution Wien: Werkausgabe 1923.

Bock S. *Mit dem Koffer in der Hand: Leben in den Wirren der Zeit 1920-1946* Wien: Passagen Verlag 1999.

Botz G. *Nationalsozialismus in Wien: Machtübernahme und Herrschaftssicherung 1938/39* Buchloe:dvo 1988.

Braunthal J. *War Resistance in Austria and Germany* in *We did not fight*. London: Cobden Sanderson 1935.

Brock P. *Pacifism in Europe to 1914.* Princetown N.J.: Princetown University Press 1972.

Brown C.C. *Building and Discovery* London: Friends Service Council 1934.

Carsten F.L. *The First Austrian Republic 1918-1938 A Study based on British and Austrian Documents* Cambridge: Gower/ Maurice Temple Smith 1986.

Carsten F.L. *Faschismus in Osterreich: Von Schönerer zu Hitler* München: Wilhelm Frank Verlag 1977.

Clark H. *War and its Aftermath, Letters from France, Austria and the Middle East* Ed. Edith Pye, Wells, Somerset and London: Clark, Son & Co. undated.

Darton L. *Friends Committee for Refugees and Aliens 1933-1950* London: Friends House 1954,.

Enderly-Burcel G. *Protokolle des Ministerrates der Ersten Republik. Kabinett Engelbert Dollfuß vol 1, no 816* Vienna 1980-86.

Fassmann H. & Münz R. *Historische Migrationsmuster, aktuelle Trends und politische Maßnahmen* Wien: Jugend und Volk 1995.

Fogelman E. *Conscience and Courage: Rescuers of Jews during the Holocaust.* New York: Anchor 1992.

Fox H. *Quakerism in Austria* Vienna: J. Weiner undated.

Fry A.R. A Quaker Adventure London: Nisbet & Co 1926.

Gilbert M. The Holocaust: The Jewish Tragedy London: Collins 1986.

Greenwood J.O. Quaker Encounters, vol.1-3. York: William Sessions Ltd 1975;1977;1978.

Gruber H. *Red Vienna: Experiment in Working-class Culture 1919-1934* New York: OVP 1991.

Gulick C.A. *Österreich from Habsburg to Hitler* Wien: Forum Verlag 1976.

Hall W. *Quaker International Work in Europe since 1914.* Geneva: Imprimerie Reunie de Chambery 1938.

Hardy C.O. *The Housing Program of the City of Vienna* Washington: Brooklings Institute 1934.

Haslem B. *From Suffrage to Internationalism: the Political Evolution of Three British Feminists 1908-1939.* New York: Peter Lang, 1999.

Hasley G.E. and Rowntree J.S. *This Way Lies Peace* Leeds: 1938 (no publisher given).

Hastings A. *A History of English Christianity 1920-1990* London: SCM Press Ltd, 1990.

Hinshaw D. *Herbert Hoover: an American Quaker* London: Farrar, Straus & Co, 1950.

Hobhouse H. *I Appeal to Caesar* London: George Allen & Unwin, 1919

Hirst M. E. *The Quakers in Peace and War* London: Swarthmore Press, 1923.

Hoxie Jones M.J. *Swords into Ploughshares* New York: Macmillan, 1937.

Janik A. & Toulmin S.*: Wittgenstein's Vienna* London: Weidenfeld & Nicolson, 1973.

Jelavich B. *Modern Austria: Empire and Republic* Cambridge: Cambridge University Press, 1987.

Jones R. *The Trail of Life in the Middle Years* New York: Macmillan, 1934.

Kenworthy L. *An American Quaker inside Nazi Germany* Pennsilvania: Quaker Publications, 1982.

Lawson B. *Memories of a Quaker International Worker* Birmingham: privately published, 1978.

Lovell P. *Quaker Inheritance – 1871-1961* London: Bannersdale Press, 1970.

Marquis E.G. *They Kept the Faith* Edinburgh: privately published, 1990.

Midlarsky E. *Competence and Helping: Notes towards a model* in: *Development and Maintenance of Prosocial Behaviour; International Perspectives on Positive Morality.* New York: Plenum 1984.

Monk R. *Wittgenstein- the Duty of Genius.* London: Vintage, 1990.

Nicolson H. *Peacemaking 1919:* Berlin: S. Fischer Verlag, 1933.

Oldfield S. ed. *This Working World: Women's Lives and Culture(s) in Britain 1914-1945* London: Taylor & Francis, 1994.

Otto, H. *Werden und Wesen des Quäkertums und seine Entwicklung in Deutschland* Vienna: Sensen Verlag, 1972.

Parker J. *The Jewish Problem in the Modern World* London: Thornton Butterworth Ltd, 1939.

Reynolds R. *Quaker Biographies: John S. Hoyland* London: Friends Home Service Committee, 1958.

Reichhold L. *Kampf um Österreich: Die Vaterländische Front und ihr Widerstand gegen den Anschluss 1933-1938. Eine Dokumentation.* Vienna: Dokumentationsarchiv des Österreichischen Widerstandes. 1984.

Ritter H.R. *Hermann Neubacher and the German Occupation of the Balkans, 1940-45* University of Virginia, 1969.

Roberts J.M. *Europe* London: Longman, 1989.

Roberts S. H. *The House that Hitler Built* London: Methuen 1937.

Rosenkranz H. *Verfolgung und Selbstbehauptung - die Juden in Österreich* Wien/München: Harold, 1978.

Schausberger N. *Der Griff nach Österreich: Der "Anschluß"* Wien-München: Jugend und Volk, 1988.

Scheu F. *Der Weg ins Ungewisse: Österreichs Schicksalskurve 1929-1938* Wien: Fritz Molden Verlag, 1972.

Shirer W.L. *Berlin Diary* London: Hanish Hamilton, 1941

Schmitt H.A. *Quakers & Nazis* Columbia/London: University of Mitchigan Press, 1997.

Sereny G. *Albert Speer: His Battle with Truth* London: Picador, 1995.

Sessions W. K. *They Chose the Star,* York: Sessions Book Trust, revised edition 1991.

Seton-Watson R.W. *Britain and the Dictator* Cambridge: Cambridge University Press, 1938.

Speiser W. *Paul Speiser und das Rote Wien* Vienna: Jugend und Volk, 1979.

Stadler K. R. *Austria* London: Ernst Benn Ltd, 1971.

Opfer verlorener Zeiten: Geschichte der Schutzbund-Emigration 1934 Wien: Europaverlag, 1974.

Stolzfus N. *Resistance of the Heart* New York: Norton & Co, 1996.

Tacke K. ed. *Lebensbilder deutscher Quäker während der NS-Herrschaft 1933-1945* Bad Pyrmont: Deutsche Jahresversammlung, 1992.

Taylor A.J.P. *A Survey of the Development of Germany since 1815* London: Hamish Hamilton, 1945.

Tritton F.J. *Carl Heath – Apostle of peace* London: Friends Home Service Committee, n.d.

Vining, E. G. *Friend of Life- a Biography of Rufus Jones* London: Michael Joseph, 1959.

Weidenfeld G. *Remembering My Good Friends* London: Harper Collins, 1995.

Wilkinson W. *Students Make their Lives* London: George Allen & Unwin Ltd, 1935.

Wilson F.M. *In the Margins of Chaos* London: John Murray, 1944.

Rebel Daughter of a Country House London: George Allen & Unwin Ltd, 1967.

Wyman D. S. *The Abandonment of the Jews. America and the Holocaust:* London: Pantheon 1984.

Zöllner E. *Österreich: Sein Werden in der Geschichte* Wien-St Pölten: Welt und Heimat, 1961.

Periodicals and Reports:

Gildermeister M.L. *American Relief and Reconstruction Work in Austria 1918-1923* Haverford: Haverford College Library 1945.

FE&WVRC Leaflet 83 *Statement of Accounts.*

FE&WVRC Leaflet 84 *A Challenge: Is This Your Concern?*

Foreign Membership Papers: Friends House Library.

Friends' Fellowship Papers London: July 1921.

Friends' Service Council Annual Reports 1928-38.

Friends' Quarterly Magazine London: 1923.

Handbook of the Religious Society of Friends Philadelphia 1941.

Journal of the Friends' Historical Society Volume 56 Number 1 1990.

Judenplatz: Place of Remembrance. Wien: Pichler Verlag, 2000.

Reports of the German Emergency Committee (joint committee of Meeting for Sufferings and Friends Service Council).

Reports of the *All Friends Conference* London: 1920.
Reports of the *Joint Meeting of C.I.S. and FE&WVRC* 10th May 1921.
Reports of the *Foreign Membership Committee of C.I. S.* 31st May 1920.
The Friend: *a Religious, Literary and Miscellaneous Journal* London: 5th September 1919; 13th March 1920; 25th June 1920; 11th February 1921; 8th April 1921; 27th April 1921; 28th October 1921; 9th December 1921; 13th October 1934.

Archive Material

Alexander Horace, Personal Files no. 1: Woodbrooke Library, Birmingham.

Cadbury Emma, Correspondence 1938-39: Haverford College Special Collection, Haverford PA.

Clark Roger, Journals on visits to Vienna 1919-1922: Clark Family Archives, Street, Somerset.

Clark Hilda, Letters and Journals: Clark Family Archives, Street, Somerset.

Correspondence exchanged between AFSC and Vienna 1919-41. American Friends Service Committee.

Greenwood J.O., unpublished manuscript: Woodbrooke Library, Birmingham.

Horsenaill H., *The Vienna International Centre* unpublished manuscript: Friends' House Library, London:.

Hoyland J.S. et al. *Building by Pick and Shovel* unpublished Manuscript: Woodbrooke Library, Birmingham.

Seutemann File, Friends House Library, London.

Interviews and Correspondence

Brenda Bailey; Antonia Bruha; Ben Buxton; Tessa Cadbury; J. Roger Carter; Dennis Conolly; Marlis Gildermeister; Nicolas Gillett; Frederika Heller; Susanne Jalkotzy; Ruth Karrach; Veronika Kothbauer; Chris Lawson; Gillian Lewitt; Percy Lovell; Graham Marquis; Rosalind Priestman; Drusilla Pye; John Sheldon; Grete Scherer; Hans A. Schmitt.

Index of Names

ALBRECHT, Hans, xi, 85, 86, 88, 101, 102, 108, 119, 122, 130, 131, 135, 136, 145, 146, 155-7, 159
Alexander, Horace, 63, 65, 66, 74, 168
Anderson, Margaret, 21, 22, 24, 25, 32, 37, 38
Andrews, Helen, 114
Appel, Friederike, 36

BACKHOUSE, Edward, 25, 37, 68
Barrow, Florence, 129, 138
Bauer, Otto, 21, 69, 164
Bayer, Frau, 69
Bell, Jane, 57, 59
Bellamy, Ellen, 57
Bettelheim, Bruno, 124, 138
Biddle, Clement, 28, 29
Böck, Katharina, 56
Böck, Rudi, x, 72, 84, 91, 93, 95, 100-2, 107, 119, 127-35, 139, 140, 142, 155, 161, 162
Böck, Rudolf, x, 54, 55, 58-60, 69, 74, 110
Böck-Schnellar, Grete, 97
Böhme, Jakob, 102
Bracey, Bertha, 116, 119
Brown, Christine Clement, 36, 39, 53, 62, 71, 72, 74, 164
Bruha, Antonia, 136, 139, 163, 168
Bürckel, Josef, 129
Buxton, Ben, 20, 168

CADBURY, Emma, x, xi, 60, 78, 79, 81, 83, 84, 86, 87, 91, 106, 108, 109, 111-3, 115-7, 119, 120, 124, 126, 129, 138, 140, 147, 156, 162, 168

Cadbury, George, 36
Campbell, Mary, 95, 108, 113, 119, 122, 137, 139
Carter, J. Roger, 108, 119, 130, 147, 168
Catchpool, Corder, 84, 105, 108, 110, 119, 130
Chamberlain, Neville, 131
Churchill, Winston, 1, 127
Clark, Alice, 19, 29, 38, 42
Clark, Hilda, x, xi, 4-7, 9, 11-3, 15, 16, 18-20, 22-4, 26, 29-38, 43, 49, 55, 57, 68, 78, 79, 90, 108, 115, 116
Clark, Roger, 17, 30, 105
Clark, William Stephens, 4, 19
Courtney, Kathleen, 22, 37
Cunninghame, Sir Thomas, 7, 16

DOLLFUSS, Alwine, 79
Dollfuss, Engelbert, 76-80, 84, 85, 124, 134

ECKHARD, Meister, 102
Eichmann, Adolf, 115
Elkington, Howard, 119, 144-6, 155
Ellis, Marion, 43

FESTINGER, Leon, 133, 139
Fey, Emil, 77
Fox, George, 46, 101
Fox, Helen, 9, 43-8, 51, 53-6, 69, 70
Freud, Sigmund, 33, 34
Fry, Joan, 48, 49

GHEEL-GILDERMEESTER, Frank von, 112
Gillett, Rowntree, 68

Goebbels, Joseph, 102, 133
Goleman, Daniel, 148, 158
Greenwood, John Ormerod, 19-21, 37-9, 48, 50, 51, 63, 74, 120, 162, 165, 168
Guttwillinger, Ottilie, 72, 90, 92, 124

HALIFAX, Lord, 127
Harris, Redford, 60
Harvey, T. Edmund, 5, 20
Haughton, Ethel, 109, 113, 116, 120, 121
Heath, Carl, x, xi, 41-4, 46-50, 55-7, 59-61, 63, 66-8, 72-4, 85, 86, 100, 102, 167
Hedin, Sven, 127
Heydrich, Reinhard, 148
Hitler, Adolf, 76, 84, 95, 97, 99, 102-6, 110, 111, 115, 127-9, 131, 136, 157, 164-6
Hodgkin, Henry, 41, 49
Hoover, Herbert, 8, 135, 165
Horsenaill, Headley, xi, 21, 39, 55, 57-60, 63, 65, 68, 70, 72, 74, 79, 85, 87, 89-91, 97, 106, 107, 117, 168
Hoxie Jones, Mary, 120, 139, 145-7, 159, 165
Hoyland J. S., 91, 166, 168
Hughes, William, 110

INNITZER, Theodor, 79, 108

JACOB, Louise M., 108
Jahoda, Maria, 92
Jalkotzy, Alois, 54, 77, 91, 93, 95, 127, 130, 138, 140, 142, 161, 162
Jebb, Eglantyne, 15, 16
Jonas, Franz, 81
Jones, Margaret, 140-7, 162
Jones, Rufus, 46, 48, 85, 86, 132, 134, 167
Jordan, Henrietta (Mizi), 159
Jung, C. G., 33

KAFKA, Frau, 87

Karrach, Ruth, 117, 120, 121, 168
Kenworthy, Leonard, 129, 138, 146, 149, 158, 165
Kreisler, Dr, 124, 125
Kun, Bela, 7

LACHMUND, Margarete, 159
Langenfeld, Ernst, 69, 70
Lawson, Bernard, 13, 20, 88, 89, 101, 105, 108, 122, 126, 130, 131, 137, 138, 142, 160, 162, 163, 165
Lihotsky, Grete, 27, 38
Lipovsky, Franz, 136, 140, 144, 152, 156, 159
Lloyd George, David, 13, 127
Loos, Adolf, 27, 38

MACMASTER, Gilbert, 110
Marquis, Graham, 93, 98, 105, 165, 168
Martin, Anne, 103, 105
McMaster, Gilbert, 85, 86
Munro, Dr Henry, 16
Murray, Agnes, 17, 21
Mussolini, Benito, 76, 84, 104

NEUBACHER, Hermann, 128, 129, 166
Neumayer, Käthe, x, 87, 113, 120, 136, 140, 141, 143-7, 149, 152, 156, 157, 162

ORMEROD, Mary, 111
Otto-Ottenfeld, Wilhelmine, 108

PAPANEK, Ernst, 116, 117, 121
Pickett, Clarence, 89, 125, 131, 132, 138, 146, 147
Pirquet, Clemens von, 5, 60
Pye, Edith, 6, 11, 19, 20, 31, 42, 78, 164

RENNER, Karl, 109, 119
Roosevelt, President, 111
Rowntree, Maurice, 9, 43, 45, 50

SAMUEL, Lord, 116

Scheu, Friedrich, 79, 81, 83, 166
Scheu, Gustav, 33
Scheu-Riess, Helene, 33, 36, 47
Schevenels, Walter, 79
Schindler, Albine, 161
Schindler, Hans, 56, 57, 64, 65, 70
Schindler, Joseph, 70
Schmidt, Herbert, 67, 68
Schmitt, Hans, x, 120, 133, 139, 147, 166, 168
Schubert, Willi, 65-7
Schuschnigg, Kurt, 84, 99, 104, 106, 124, 127, 134
Sereny, Gitta, 127, 138, 166
Seutemann, Cilli, 149, 150, 154, 157-60, 168
Seyss-Inquart, Arthur, 104
Shaw, George Bernard, 127
Shirer, William L., 103, 105, 166
Smuts, Jan Christiaan, 7, 8, 20
Spohrer, Jolante, 155
Stalin, Josif, 81
Steere, Douglas, xi, 145, 147, 155
Stein, Gertrude, 127
Steiner, Edward C., 49
Steiner, Rudolf, 57
Stewart, Ann, 108
Sumpf, Grete, x, 142-5, 147, 149-60

TAYLOR, Alonzo E., 8, 167
Telheim, Adele, 154, 155
Telheim, Steffi, 154
Thomas, Anna M., 47, 48

UNRUH, Professor, 85

WEISS, Dr, 38, 45
Wilson, Francesca, x, 9, 14, 18, 20, 21, 25, 26, 31-3, 38, 39, 167
Wood, H. G., 49
Wyman, David S., 152, 158, 159, 167

YARNELL, Robert, 109, 110, 119, 132, 133, 138

ZIMMERL, Roman, 68